'If Christ be not risen...'

'If Christ be not risen...'

Essays in resurrection and survival

Editors:
John Greenhalgh, Elizabeth Russell

COLLINS

Collins Liturgical in the USA
Icehouse One – 401, 151 Union Street
San Francisco, CA 94111–1299

First published in 1986 by St Mary's, Bourne Street
USA edition published by Collins Liturgical, 1988

ISBN 0 00 599083 1

Photoset in Souvenir and Times by Uniprint Ltd., Lawn Lane, London SW8
Printed in Great Britain by Bell and Bain Ltd., Glasgow

Contents

Introduction

John Gilling

I HOPE NO ONE will be disappointed by the contents of this small book. The subtitle, *Essays in resurrection and survival*, may raise expectations of new evidence of psychical goings-on under experimental conditions or highly controversial philosophical-theological-historical arguments. But the concern of the editors is not to arouse the interest of those to whom a good academic battle is the breath of life nor to reassure the doubtful by examples of scientific necromancy. It is quite simply that eternal life is still as much a legitimate concern of Christian thought as it was in the original preaching of the faith.

I would like to thank the editors and contributors to '*If Christ be not risen* . . .' for all the work they have done to make it both a good and profitable read, and Mr. Edward Mendelson who, acting for the estate of W. H. Auden gave permission for the printing of the sermon, *Words and the Word*.

W. H. Auden gave me the manuscript of this after preaching it for College Evensong at Christ Church, Oxford, on October 24th, 1965. He did not give it to me with any intention of its being published but I am sure, though some of the material in it was expanded for the T. S. Eliot Memorial Lectures given in the University of Kent in 1967 (published by Faber and Faber as *Secondary Worlds*, 1968), it is well worth printing not only for its own merit but for its use to scholars.

In recent years Christian theology has for various reasons, partly from pressing social and political causes, partly from a desire for relevance to the ideas and values of a secular age, taken a this-worldly point of view of our religion. The resurrection and the life of the world to come have been relegated to the lumber room or the old curiosity shop as dusty notions from the Church's past; it is as if we had forgotten that death exists or refused to consider it, pushing it aside as a thing too painful to bring to mind; it is as if we did not dare to believe in the eternity of the love of God like long-term prisoners who can no longer bear the thought of freedom. I hope these essays will do something to redress the balance of our understanding of the gospel.

John Gilling is parish priest of St Mary's, Bourne Street.

The keystone of Christian faith

John Macquarrie

SCEPTICAL PHILOSOPHERS sometimes challenge theologians to say just what would cause them to give up their faith. Is there any doctrine which, if it were conclusively falsified, would lead the believer to say that he could be a believer no longer? It would be as if one had pulled the keystone out of an arch, so that the whole surrounding structure collapsed.

The title of this book[1], taken from the great fifteenth chapter of St Paul's First Letter to the Corinthians, shows us how the apostle would have responded to such a challenge. 'If Christ has not been raised,' he writes, 'then our preaching is in vain and your faith is in vain!' He is claiming that the resurrection of Jesus Christ from the dead is central to Christian faith. If you take away the resurrection, then both proclamation and faith become empty and pointless exercises.

Living as we do in an age of reductionism, when many theologians think that the Christian faith must be secularised and made as inoffensive as possible, we may think that Paul has been somewhat reckless in making everything depend on the reality of Christ's resurrection. Is not that one of the weakest and most vulnerable articles in the creed? In this enlightened modern age, surely everyone knows that dead men do not rise. To say that Christian faith stands or falls with the resurrection of our Lord is to offer an unbearable offence to the modern mind. Incidentally, it seems to have been an offence to the ancient mind too, for when Paul preached on the resurrection at Athens, the sophisticated people there laughed at him. They knew as well as people know today that dead men do not rise.

Would it not then have been much safer and simpler if Paul had said that Christianity stands or falls by the beauty of Christ's moral teaching or the integrity of his character or something else that is acceptable to the liberal secularised mind? Yes, it would have been safer, but it would not have been very exciting and it would not have made many converts to the new faith. The Danish philosopher Kierkegaard, writing in the aftermath of the Enlightenment, pointed to the fact that the passion with which men and women commit themselves to Christianity is proportionate to the offence and paradox which it offers. Where everything is explained and made acceptable so that Christianity is no more than what reasonable people have always believed from the beginning of civilisation, then it is deprived of interest and is no longer something to get excited or passionate about. Resurrection may be something very difficult to believe and an offence to the rationalist, but at least one can say that it is a really stupendous idea. If Christ has risen, then something has happened that is of first-class significance for every human being, something that should stir us to the very depths. But if Christ be not risen, if he is no more than the rabbi of Nazareth, one more in the long line of religious teachers, then there is no need to get excited about him. We may respect him, as we respect Moses or Socrates, but it would be nonsense to give him the exalted position which he has always had in the Christian Church, nonsense to acclaim him as Saviour and Lord, nonsense to pray through him to the Father, nonsense to celebrate the Eucharist. The keystone would be pulled out, and the whole Christian edifice as we have known it would collapse.

Let us remember too that, although it was St Paul who used the forthright words, 'If Christ has not been raised, then our preaching is in vain and your faith is in vain,' he was simply expressing a belief that was shared by all the earliest Christians. The Church would never have come into existence if there had not been a company of men and women who were utterly and passionately convinced that Jesus had been raised from the dead and was still among them to lead them on. It is, I would argue, a historical certainty as solid as any that the birth of the Church depended on the disciples' belief in the resurrection of their

Master. Of course, their belief may have been mistaken – that is a question we shall have to examine. But we can begin from the solid fact that only a belief that Christ had risen and lives on provides anything like a sufficient reason for the rise of Christianity. That is the justification for St Paul's assertion that if Christ has not been raised, Christianity is empty and illusory.

★   ★   ★

The next step is to try to clarify what we mean when we use the word 'resurrection'. We have already noted that in both modern and ancient times, the claim that someone had risen from the dead is likely to be received with scepticism. Dead men do not rise – or so people believe. Yet, alongside this widespread scepticism and sense of the finality of death, there has been an equally widespread hope that there is life beyond death. Even in prehistoric times, the care that was taken in the burial of the dead gives testimony of a hope that these deceased had not just disappeared into nothing. In the great civilisation of ancient Egypt there was, at least among the upper classes, intense preoccupation with the life to come. Human life on this earth is always in the midst of projects that are still on the way to fulfilment, and so it is when there comes the moment of death. We are still in the midst and still looking forward, so it is natural to hope beyond death. Even today, in spite of all the secularisation and the preoccupation with material things, people have difficulty in coming to terms with death and venture to hope that life in some form goes on beyond.

The hope for a life beyond death has, historically, taken two main forms. One developed in Greece and was given a philosophical formulation by Socrates and Plato. These thinkers envisaged the immortality of the soul. The body, they taught, eventually dies and disintegrates, but the soul is by nature immortal and has neither beginning nor end. This belief tended to make those who held it despise the body. The real person, they believed, is the soul and death is an escape from the body with all its earthiness and its temptations. The other main form of belief in a life to come had its origins in Jewish religion. Jews believed that, since the body is created by God, it is, like the whole material creation, good, and so they held that the body too will have its place in any life beyond death. So their belief was in a resurrection of the body, rather than in the continuing existence of the soul without the body.

This Jewish belief in resurrection had taken a long time to develop. In the oldest parts of the Hebrew scriptures, there is no clear belief in a life beyond death. It is true that the Hebrews believed that the ghost or shade of a dead person went down to the underworld, which they called Sheol, but this was a place of gloom where the departed had only a minimal half-existence, if one may so speak. But, if one believes in a God whose purposes for his creatures are good, can one be content to suppose that nothing better awaits them than to linger on in the dusty twilight existence of Sheol? That question became acute for the Jews at the time of the Maccabean wars, about which you can read in the deutero-canonical books, sometimes called the Apocrypha. The land of Israel had been invaded by pagan conquerors, who sought by the most brutal means to stamp out the ancient faith of Israel and to force the Jews to become pagans like themselves. The Jews put up a heroic resistance, and many of their young men perished in the defence of their faith. What was to become of those martyrs whose lives had been cut off so abruptly? Surely, people reasoned, if there is a just God in heaven, he will vindicate those who have laid down their lives rather than depart from the ancient faith? Surely there must be something better than Sheol? Not a shadowy half-existence but a fuller life than even they had known in the days of their health and prosperity on earth would be the only fitting destiny for those who had endured torture and death for the sake of their faith in the one God. And such a fuller life, they believed, must include the body, resurrected from the dead.

At first glance, it might seem that a belief in the resurrection of the body is more primitive and less intellectually defensible than the Greek philosophers' teaching about the immortality of the soul. But this is not so. After all, it is through the body that we are inserted into a world where we can both act and be acted upon. It is through the body also that we are able to communicate with one another. If we had no bodies, we could not see or hear or touch or speak. It has been suggested that a disembodied soul would be restricted to its own memories and that even these would eventually fade in its solitary existence. That, of course, can be only a speculation. But it suggests that the Jews were right in looking for a resurrection of the body, for only so could the life to come have the fullness and concreteness of a truly personal existence. The life of a disembodied spirit would be more like the ghostly existence of Sheol or Hades. However, in the history of Christian theology, there has been some ambivalence and the distinction between immortality of the soul and resurrection has not always been clearly maintained. Even in the case of the resurrection of our Lord, the New Testament associates the risen Lord and the Holy Spirit so closely that sometimes it is very difficult to distinguish them. There are some problems here, to which I shall return, but perhaps it is enough for the present simply to point to the fact that any fully personal existence must be an embodied existence, and that a doctrine of resurrection safeguards this point. As Dr Mascall has recently written, 'The bodily resurrection of Jesus implies the full reintegration of his human nature, and with that reintegration its transformation and glorification.'[2] So far is a doctrine of resurrection from being primitive or indefensible compared with a doctrine of the immortality of the soul that it is only resurrection that can offer a worthwhile life beyond death, that is, a true reintegration of the whole person in all its relationships. I think then we must hold fast to the notion of bodily resurrection as contrasted with a purely spiritual immortality, but we have still to inquire more deeply just what resurrection means.

★   ★   ★

Returning to St Paul, we find him writing, 'But someone will ask, "How are the dead raised? With what kind of body do they come?"' 'Perhaps these questions are simply unanswerable while we are living as mortal creatures of perishable flesh and blood. Yet we have a duty to try to answer them to the fullest extent of our capacities, both that our own faith may be strengthened through a fuller understanding of what we believe, and also so that we can commend that faith to others who have doubts and perplexities over this central Christian assertion that God has raised Jesus from the dead. The idea of resurrection, implying as it does the mysterious interaction of the material and the spiritual, yes, even of the human and the divine, lies at the uttermost edge of what our finite minds can grasp, and it would be foolish and arrogant to suggest that we can have any clear or complete understanding. But the Christian faith does not arbitrarily impose upon us beliefs that are nonsensical or unintelligible. This faith has arisen out of God's gracious self-communication to us and by the patient study of it (the study which we call theology) we can advance in the understanding of divine truth.

So, let us face these questions. 'How are the dead raised? With what kind of body do they come?' I think that a little reflection makes it clear to us that the kind of body with which they come is not the mortal body of flesh and blood and bone and carbon chemistry that we know in our life here on earth. That body is like a motor car – it has a built-in obsolescence. It may keep going for seventy or eighty or even a hundred years, but at last, necessarily, it will wear out and death will take place. So resurrection, as Christian faith proclaims it, cannot be anything so simple as the resuscitation of a corpse, for that could be only a temporary restoration of life, and death would eventually supervene. Or, to put the same point in a different way, there is a vast difference between the resurrection of Jesus Christ and, let us say, the raising of Lazarus. Lazarus was revived in his mortal body, but presumably he died in the course of time, probably 'full of years' and not cut off prematurely, as his first death seems to have been. But Jesus Christ in his resurrection had conquered death, he is now 'alive for evermore'. A perishable body of flesh and blood could not be the bearer of this eternal death-transcending existence. It would be only a body which had undergone, in the words of Dr Mascall, already quoted, 'transformation and glorification'. This is the teaching we find in St Paul, though in different words. The body which is sown (in death) is not the body which is to be. God will give the body which he has chosen, for, we are told, there are many kinds of body. What is sown is perishable, but what is raised is imperishable. The apostle goes on. 'It is sown in weakness, it is raised in power. It is sown a physical body, it is raised a spiritual body. If there is a physical body, there is also a spiritual body.'

All of this throws light on our questions about how the dead are raised and with what bodies they come. There is confirmation here that resurrection is not to be equated with the mere reviving of the dead body, but is rather a transformation or transfiguration into another mode of being which, however, is still bodily – a spiritual body, St Paul calls it, although it is not easy to see what this expression 'spiritual body' means. We have to get away from thinking that the word 'body' means merely or even primarily the familiar structure of flesh, bones, blood, and the like. Rather, the body is that aspect of one's being whereby one is inserted into a world and so empowered to perceive, communicate and act in that world. The fleshly body is the kind of body by which we are inserted into this material world of space and time. But it is conceivable that there are other worlds which we could only enter with a different kind of body, and it may be something like this that the apostle had in mind when he insisted that there are different kinds of bodies, each with its appropriate dignity or glory. At any rate, he seems to be clear that the risen body is not simply the physical body revived, and although the popular Christian conception of resurrection has often understood it as a literal revivification of a corpse, many theologians of both ancient and modern times have followed St Paul in distinguishing a physical and a spiritual body, and in claiming that the resurrection body belongs in the latter category. Thus Origen, writing in the early part of the third century, says, 'Neither we nor the divine scriptures maintain that those long dead will rise up from the earth and live in the same bodies without undergoing any change for the better.'[3] I believe too that it is something like this that David Jenkins, the controversial Bishop of Durham, has been trying to say in recent times, though unfortunately he has not expressed himself clearly, so that people have heard the denial that the risen body is the mortal physical body but have not heard the affirmative assertion that it is a transformed and glorious body of the kind we may call a 'spiritual body'. Of course, it must also be said that there is some continuity between these bodies, for they are both constitutive of the same enduring person.

Let us try to probe further into the meaning of this expression, 'spiritual body'. Although we often speak of body and soul as if these were two quite different entities which are nevertheless somehow joined together in the living person, I think that both the biblical understanding of a human person and the modern understanding of such a person holds him or her to be a unity within which there are two aspects, a spiritual aspect and a bodily aspect. These are distinguishable but not separable – a point which we noted when we saw how the Jews opted for a doctrine of resurrection rather than one which claimed immortality only for the soul. This unitary view of the human person is sometimes expressed by saying that man is a psychosomatic unity. The whole body is not only alive but is 'ensouled' though this may be a matter of degree and may vary in intensity from one person to another. Could we suppose that where resurrection has taken place, the degree and intensity of the impregnation and ennoblement of the material aspect of the person has reached that pitch at which one may justifiably speak of a 'spiritual body'? Would this be the kind of body to which the gospel stories of the appearances of the risen Lord to his disciples refer?

Here, of course, we have entered upon speculative territory, but I do not think the speculations are groundless. One can point to some analogies in human experience which are reasonably well attested and which may throw some light on the resurrection of the Lord. It has often been reported that persons close to God have shone with light, as if a transformation or transfiguration were already going on in them. When Moses came down from the mountain where he had communed with God, the skin of his face is said to have been shining. Similar reports are found among the Orthodox concerning very saintly persons. Of St Sergius, after his death, it was said that 'the saint's face, unlike that of other dead, glowed with the life of the living or as one of God's angels',[4] while as late as the eighteenth century we have this report from a disciple of St Seraphim, as he conversed with him. 'I looked into his face, and there came over me an even greater reverential awe. Imagine in the centre of the sun, in the dazzling brilliance of his midday rays, the face of the man who talks with you. You see the movement of his lips and the changing expression of his eyes, you hear his voice, you feel someone grasp your shoulders; yet you do not see the hands, you do not see yourself or his figure, but only a blinding light...'[5] The reader will notice the resemblance between this experience and Paul's meeting with the risen Christ on the Damascus road. It is almost as if, in the case of Moses and of the Russian saints mentioned, resurrection, the transfiguration and glorification of the body, had already begun. So enveloped were they and permeated by the Spirit of God that they could be said to be living in God and God in them – 'partakers of the divine nature' as one New Testament writer expresses it.

There are other analogies which help us to grasp how in the 'spiritual body' (if we are rightly interpreting this idea) the distinction between body and spirit seems to disappear in a new integrated reality. One thinks, for instance, of the claim of the mystic, Richard Rolle, that he experienced the love of God in his soul like a physical warmth. He did not think that this was only a figure of speech. He says, 'I cannot tell you how surprised I was the first time I felt my heart begin to be warm. It was real warmth, too, not imaginary, and it felt as if it were really on fire.'[6]

There is still another related type of experience which helps to illuminate these matters. Some mystics have spoken of the 'spiritual senses', powers of perception analogous to the bodily senses of sight, hearing, touch and so on, but able to perceive realities which escape the ordinary 'dullness of our blinded

sight'. These spiritual senses have been recently discussed by
Hans Urs von Balthasar in his great work, *The Glory of the
Lord,* devoted to the neglected theme of theological aesthetics.[7]
He cites a long series of Christian writers, including Origen, St
Augustine, St Bonaventure, St Ignatius Loyola and in our own
time Karl Barth, all of whom speak of a mode of heightened
perception in which they establish a relation to spiritual
realities. St Augustine, for instance, could speak of seeing,
hearing, even touching God. 'There my soul receives a radiance
that no space can grasp; there something sounds which no time
can take away; there something gives a fragrance that no wind
can dissipate; there something is savoured which no satiety can
make bitter; there something is embraced which can occasion no
boredom.'[8] This is the language of a visionary, yet it is not
merely subjective language. It is not a purely spiritual language
either, but a sensory language. Does it not spring from the
mysterious constitution of the human being in whom sense and
intellect, soul and body, spirit and matter, are integrated? Do
we not meet here once again a suggestion of the 'spiritual body'?
Is not the integration of the spiritual and the physical perfected
in the resurrection of Jesus Christ?

★ ★ ★

Up to this point, I have been concerned mainly to clarify the
meaning of resurrection. This attempt has admittedly led us into
some rather speculative ideas, yet they are not fantastic
speculations but have analogies in our human experience and so
they can help us to understand better what we mean when we
affirm that Christ has risen, and Christian faith is strengthened
as we enter more deeply into the understanding of it. But even
if we have succeeded in making clearer our belief in the
resurrection, we have still to ask whether it is true. What
grounds have we for believing that Jesus Christ has risen from
the dead?

There are two different kinds of grounds. One is *testimony,* the reports of the earliest generation of Christians that they had seen the risen Lord or had some other evidence which they interpreted as meaning that he had risen from the dead. These reports are now contained in the New Testament, and while it might be very difficult to say of any particular example that it is an eye-witness account, nevertheless they come from a very early stratum of tradition and are proof of the point made at the beginning of this article that these early Christians were 'utterly and passionately convinced' that Jesus had risen from the dead, and that without this conviction the Church would never have come into being. Of course, as I said, these early believers might have been mistaken and they might have misinterpreted their experiences. If so, Christian beliefs about Jesus rest on error, and, as Paul so frankly acknowledged, one then has to say that the faith is vain. That is a problem we shall have to consider. The other kind of ground on which one might believe that Jesus rose from the dead is our own *present experience*. If he is alive for evermore, then people of later times can still meet him in his risen power, not perhaps in the dramatic way in which he appeared to the twelve, but nonetheless in ways which still carry conviction. Do we, as baptised Christians, know what it means to be risen with Christ and to be members of his living body? On this last point, let me straight away dispose of one interpretation of the resurrection, which I think is totally inadequate. This is the belief that Christ has risen in the Church, that the Church itself is his risen body. A more specific version of this view was taught by Rudolf Bultmann, who claimed that it is in the proclamation of the Church that Christ lives on and his word still summons men and women to the decision of faith. This is all true and important. But it will not do if it is meant to be a sufficient account of what is meant by the resurrection of Christ. The early Church did not create its new life out of its own resources or out of its nostalgic memories of a dead teacher. It lived in the power of the risen Lord, a Lord whose own rising was prior to the rising of the Church and the necessary condition for it. I suppose that many fine people can be said to live on for a time after their deaths, in their children or in their friends, because something of themselves has passed into these others and deeply influenced them. But Jesus's relation to this disciples was much more than that. He did not survive only as a gradually fading memory, but as the very source of the Church's new life.

But let us now turn to examine the testimony of the early Christians. First of all, there is the story of the empty tomb. That the tomb of Jesus was found empty is attested by all four gospels, though it is not mentioned by St Paul, who finds the appearances alone sufficient to establish the resurrection of the Lord – no doubt especially the appearance to himself on his journey to Damascus. It is true that the gospels differ among themselves in the details they give of the tomb incident – the number of women who went to the tomb and their names, the precise time of day, the angelic figures whom they saw, and what was said to them. I do not think these discrepancies are important – one would be much more suspicious if each evangelist had said exactly the same, as if there had been collusion among them. But the *theological* significance of the story comes through very clearly. It is expressed in the words, 'He is not here! He is risen!' Jesus is not to be sought among the dead, he does not end up in the tomb or in the ghostly shadows of Sheol. He lives on, and has already gone ahead to lead his disciples into mission.

Protestant scholars have tended to be dismissive of the story of the empty tomb. Perhaps like Paul they have relied simply on the appearance stories, or perhaps they have thought that even if the tomb was found empty, there are several ways in which this could be interpreted. Bultmann believed that the story of the empty tomb is a later legend, invented to provide some objective ballast to the appearance stories, which he regarded as accounts of subjective experience. Pannenberg is an exception to the general scepticism. He believes that the original tradition about the resurrection had two strands, the appearances *and* the empty tomb, and that although the latter is not mentioned by St. Paul, it is not therefore without significance, and, taken in conjunction with the appearances, is most naturally interpreted in terms of resurrection. But to find someone among contemporary writers who places the full weight on the empty tomb as the primary ground for the rise of belief in the resurrection, we must go to Geza Vermes, the reader in Jewish

Studies at Oxford University. He writes, 'In the end, when every argument has been considered and weighed, the only conclusion acceptable to the historian must be that the opinions of the orthodox, the liberal sympathiser, and the critical agnostic alike – and even perhaps of the disciples themselves – are simply interpretations of the one disconcerting fact: that the women who set out to pay their last respects to Jesus found, to their consternation, not a body but an empty tomb.'[9] Vermes goes on to point out that there could be various reasons for the fact of the tomb's being empty, and that this fact *by itself* would scarcely constitute strong evidence for a resurrection.

But, of course, it does not stand by itself. It has to be considered along with the appearances of Jesus to the disciples, and these appearances constitute the major evidence for the resurrection. It is true that sceptics might allege (and have alleged) that the disciples' experience of seeing, hearing and even touching the risen Christ was a purely subjective type of experience, even hallucination, which is the word used by the American theologian, Gordon Kaufman. But Kaufman goes on to say that 'the negative connotations to our modern ears of words like "vision" or "hallucination" should not be allowed to call into question the ultimate validity of what was communicated in and what occurred through these events.'[10] In other words, they were not mere subjective illusions, but ways by which God communicates with his creatures, and therefore open, we may suppose, to the kind of interpretation which I sketched out in an earlier part of this article when investigating what is meant by the 'spiritual body' and the 'spiritual senses'. We have also to remember that the weight of the evidence suggests that the disciples were not expecting a resurrection. When the women first announced that Jesus had risen, their reports were dismissed as incredible. Only if the disciples had been expecting a resurrection would it be plausible to say that the appearances were nothing but wish-fulfilling illusions.

There is also current among theologians a third theory of how the disciples came to believe that Christ had risen from the dead. This is the view formulated by the well known Belgian Dominican, Edward Schillebeeckx.[11] He believes that already during the ministry of Jesus, before the crucifixion and resurrection, the disciples had come to believe in him as the prophet who was to be sent from God and who would be, as it were, a new Moses. The disciples scattered after the crucifixion and, at first, that seemed to be the end. But some of them, especially Peter, studied the scriptural teaching about the promised prophet, and came to believe that God would vindicate him and raise him up even from death. So these scattered disciples eventually came together again, already believing on the basis of their scriptural meditations that God had raised his prophet from the dead. According to Schillebeeckx, the story of the empty tomb and the various reports of appearances of the risen Lord were so far from being the *grounds* for believing in the resurrection that they were the *consequences* of a belief already arrived at as a result of meditation on the scriptures. I must bluntly say that Schillebeeckx has been guilty of putting the cart before the horse in a remarkably perverse way. Of all the attempts made to offer an historical explanation of the genesis of the belief that Christ had risen, this one seems to me to be the weakest and poorest of the lot. I think it must have taken something much more dramatic and concrete than the reading of a few passages in Deuteronomy and the Wisdom of Solomon to have brought the disciples together again and to have planted in them the unshakeable belief that Jesus had risen from the dead. An empty tomb or the personal appearance of the risen Lord might have done it, but hardly the perusal of some scattered and obscure passages of scripture. In any case, if Peter and the others came back to Jerusalem already believing in the resurrection, why were they so incredulous when the women told them that Christ had risen? It is true certainly that before long the early believers began to search the scriptures for predictions of the Messiah, not only of his resurrection but also of his death, which was a scandal to the orthodox Jews. All this was clearly expounded by David Strauss a century and a half ago. But it came after the resurrection, not before. It was the resurrection which, in Paul's words, had designated Jesus as 'Son of God in power', and the subsequent search of scripture was the attempt of the Christians to justify their belief in relation to the Jewish traditions.

Alongside the testimony of those early witnesses who appealed to appearances of the Lord and to the phenomenon of the empty tomb, we have to set our own present experience. Is it not the case that in every generation of Christians, our own included, the words of the gospel or even of a sermon can sometimes impinge on us with such lively force that in and through these human words we hear ourselves addressed by the living Christ? Is it not the case that in the sacrament of the altar we know Christ present under the forms of bread and wine, just as the disciples at Emmaus knew him in the breaking of the bread? Is it not the case that in a thousand other ways Christians are aware of Christ's presence among them and are therefore aware that he who once died now lives? It is our own experience which confirms those ancient testimonies that have been handed down in the New Testament, and when we consider testimony and experience together, we can confidently affirm that Christ is risen indeed.

It was a true instinct that led St Paul to assert the centrality of Jesus's resurrection and to acknowledge that, without it, Christian faith would collapse. Thus we must resist any attempts by theologians or others to minimise or reduce our belief in the resurrection. On the other hand, we have to remember that the New Testament itself is quite reticent about the details of what happened at that first Easter, and I have acknowledged in this article that some of the ways in which I have tried to open up the understanding of resurrection are speculative, though I thought that this was justified because the clearer our understanding, the firmer our faith will be. But I believe, in the light of all that has been said above, that the essential truth of the resurrection of Jesus Christ can be distilled into three fairly simple propositions. If we hold firmly to these, then we do indeed have a true and adequate grasp of this central doctrine of the faith.

1 Christ lives on. If we seek him in the realm of the dead, we are told, 'He is not here! He is risen!' It is not necessary for us to speculate on the nature of his risen life, but we can and must say that he had been raised to a higher mode of existence,

transfigured and glorified and so has 'abolished death and brought life and immortality to light'.

2 Christian disciples already know this resurrection life in themselves. They have been incorporated into the living body of Christ and even in this earthly life they are learning the meaning of eternal life and know that they cannot be separated from God. But this new life of the Christian community is in every way secondary to and dependent on the risen Christ himself.

3 All this tells us something about God. The resurrection of Jesus Christ means that God can always bring forth the new. He can transform any human situation, however hopeless it seems. The cross speaks of God standing with us in the flux of events; the resurrection speaks of his being always ahead of events, and is thus the great ground of hope for the world.

John Macquarrie is a canon of Christ Church, Oxford, now retired.

The resurrection in liturgical life in the Orthodox church

Elizabeth Briere

THE WHOLE OF OUR LIFE in the Church is, by definition, a life in the resurrection; it is the life of those who have been baptised into Christ's death. With the resurrection of Christ, we celebrate definitively 'the death of death, the abolition of hell, the first-fruits of another life, which is eternal' (Easter Kanon): and this reality is reflected in our liturgical life.

The resurrection was not one of the many themes which was worked into our worship and transformed into prayer. It was the one, unique theme which has flooded everything with its light; the new potential for our Church and for each independent personality, which has given another dimension to life, provided the orientation of our eucharistic worship, and given an eschatological sense to our entry into the body of the Church.[1]

We are aware that in a profound sense 'the birth of God makes nature new'[2]; but we cannot help also being acutely aware of living still in a fallen world. This does not mean that either the 'unchanged' or the 'new' aspect of our existence is unreal; more specifically and importantly, it does not mean that the new life in Christ is an abstraction, a philosophical concept or a pious hope. It simply means that 'in relation to history, we have a double existence; that of historical continuity and that of eschatological discontinuity'[3] – we live *both* in time *and* beyond the resurrection, in eternity. The process of growing into the new life into which we are born at baptism involves not ignoring our existence in time but transfiguring it; and this is a process achieved through participation in the life of the Church, the body of the risen Christ – a liturgical process.

As we give ourselves over to the celebration of the resurrection and attune ourselves to the rhythm, the thinking, the prayer of the universal Church, we begin to see our own existence and the flow of history from a different point of view. Everything is illuminated and transfigured in the clear light of the presence of the risen Christ, and becomes truth and joy and life in the eschatological perspective of the Kingdom of the Lamb.[4]

The various liturgical cycles in the Church provide a means whereby the Christian learns to celebrate the resurrection and becomes 'attuned to the rhythm of the Church' – the framework within which all his experience and the whole of his life is transformed into a participation in the death and resurrection of Christ. Liturgical life is not an 'optional extra' for Christians who have the time and the taste for it; it is our natural habitat as members of Christ, 'the world in which man lives *according to his nature* as a theanthropic entity'.[5]

Our primary liturgical experience of the resurrection occurs weekly, in the feast of the Lord's day, and annually in the Paschal cycle.

★   ★   ★

Even in our purely personal life, the progress of the week has a profound symbolism. We walk amidst pain and sorrow. We encounter and grapple hand to hand with the prince of this world, with the devil and with death . . . But at last we reach the day of the Lord, the Sunday which is full of light, to be renewed and clothed in the radiant garment of purity and hope . . . Every Sunday in our lives is an illumination in the light of the resurrection, a taste of the joy and eternal lordship of Jesus crucified and risen.[6]

The week ends with the completion of creation, the Sabbath on which the Lord rested. But this is now sealed with an eighth day, the first day of the new creation, in which the Lord is risen after resting in the tomb. The day which follows the seventh no longer simply begins another seven-day cycle – it is now an opening on to eternity, and this is a reality in our liturgical experience.

One of the most thrilling aspects of the liturgical consciousness is that in it, we are delivered from the mortal yoke of time; in it, the 'nothing is new under the sun' is vanquished by the paschal life and 'all things are made new'.[7]

It may be in the depths of Lent or another fast: but once the bell rings for Vespers on Saturday evening, it is always a feast. Even people who are not coming to church will light the lamp in front of their icons at home in honour of the day. The special verses for Saturday Vespers change weekly according to the cycle of eight Tones, but any of them immediately proclaims the event central to the feast. 'Come, let us rejoice in the Lord, who has crushed the power of death and given light to the race of men: let us sing with the bodiless powers, our Creator and our Saviour, glory to thee' (Tone 7).

Matins begins in a very different atmosphere. It is a long time before anything proper to the day is sung. Regardless of where it may appear in parish usage, Matins belongs in origin, as in monastic use, to the last hours before dawn. This setting is fundamental to the character of the service. In the opening Six Psalms,[8] read by a single reader in a darkened church, the darkness of night and the exhaustion of the small hours are assimilated to death – not physical death alone, but the deadness of sin and estrangement from God. 'Lord, how are they increased that trouble me, many are they that rise against me, many a one there be that say of my soul, "There is no help for him in his God . . ." ' (Psalm 3).

These Psalms represent an extraordinarily powerful, irresistible movement out of darkness into the light. No one who comes to them saying with the Psalmist, 'my life draweth nigh unto hell . .. like unto them that are wounded and lie in the grave, out of remembrance and cut away from thy sight . . .' (Psalm 87/88) can fail to be carried with them from despair to trust and joy, 'Look how high the heaven is in comparison of the earth – so great is the Lord's mercy upon them that fear him' (Psalm 102/103).

Although the Six Psalms are proper to Matins and not to Sunday, they are of great significance. They give a framework within which the whole pattern of our daily life, our sleeping and waking, is revealed as an assurance of the faithfulness of God who rises from the dead to save us, 'I laid me down and slept, and rose up again, for the Lord sustained me' (Psalm 3).

The Six Psalms end with an assurance of the guidance of the

Holy Spirit, 'Thy good Spirit shall lead me forth into the land of righteousness' (Psalm 142/143). At once – as it were, the first fruits of this guidance – we find ourselves greeting Christ in the words of Psalm 117/118, 'The Lord is God, and hath appeared to us; blessed is he that cometh in the name of the Lord!' Each morning is a theophany, an image of the Light coming into the world; and it is with the same words that Christ is acclaimed in the Divine Liturgy, when the celebrant opens the holy doors and comes out of the altar with the chalice. It is this refrain and its verses, with all its messianic and eschatological undertones, which leads into the first text for the day – on Sunday, the troparion of the resurrection. To give an example from one of the eight Tones, 'From on high thou didst descend, O compassionate one; thou didst accept three days' burial to free us from the passions. O Lord, our life and our resurrection, glory to thee' (Tone 8).

From the cosmic reality of the resurrection, we are taken back to the sepulchre. The *eulogitaria* – verses on Psalm 118/119 – speak of the women who came to anoint Christ's body, but 'heard an angel say to them, "why count ye the living among the dead?" For, as God, he has risen from the tomb.'[9] It is a preparation for hearing at first hand the news of the resurrection in the Matins gospel, read as if from the tomb of Christ; for living through the very first, sometimes confused intimations of the great mystery which we celebrate, and bearing witness to it as we go up to venerate the gospel book. The response to the gospel of the resurrection is immediate, 'Now that we have seen Christ's resurrection, let us venerate the holy Lord Jesus, who alone is without sin . . . For, behold, through the cross joy has come to all the world . . .'

Our liturgical experience Sunday by Sunday shapes our understanding of the resurrection, our whole theological outlook. We have lived through the joy in Christ who has overcome the world, whose victory is inevitable because he is God, who by his grace has vouchsafed this victory over death to us unless we choose to reject it. 'Let the heavens rejoice, and let the earth be glad; for the Lord has shown strength with his arm; by his death, he has trampled down death. He is become the first fruits of the dead: from the belly of hell he has delivered us, bestowing on the world great mercy' (Troparion, Tone 3). We have also experienced the infinitely mysterious character of the cross and resurrection. No amount of historical detail could explain the meaning of these events, yet as members of the Church, we live so near to them; in our own lifetime, we have seen them and understood. 'Lord, while the grave was sealed . . . thou didst come forth from the tomb as thou hadst been born of the Mother of God. Thy bodiless angels knew not how thou wast incarnate: the soldiers guarding thee did not perceive when thou didst rise. For both wonders are sealed to those who inquire, but are made manifest to those who venerate the mystery in faith . . . ' (Lauds, Tone 5).

The prime occasion for the Christian to 'venerate in faith the mystery' of Christ's incarnation, death and resurrection is, of course, the Divine Liturgy. This above all is, 'the "acceptable time" (2 Corinthians 6.2), the mysterious, charismatic opportunity offered personally to the members of the Church and to the whole body as a unity, "to know him and the power of his resurrection and the participation in his sufferings" (Philippians 3,10).'[10] The day of the resurrection has always been the primary day for the Church's eucharistic gathering, but the Liturgy does not speak much *about* the resurrection: it manifests it. 'Within the Liturgy, everything has been changed for the better, tested – that is, broken and restored – through the cross and the resurrection . . . The Divine Liturgy baptises man, nature and time with fire and the Holy Spirit. And what emerge are saints, paradise and eternity.'[11]

The Liturgy is our participation in the heavenly worship of the risen Christ, 'in a mystery representing the cherubim, and singing the thrice-holy hymn to the life-giving Trinity'. It is the time when, while still on earth, we 'taste of the well of immortality' (Communion Hymn), which is none other than 'the fountain of incorruption, welling up from the grave of Christ' (Easter Kanon).

★　★　★

Yesterday I was buried with thee, O Christ; let me rise today with thy resurrection. I was crucified with thee yesterday; do thou thyself glorify me with thee in thy Kingdom (Easter Kanon).

This verse from Easter night surely summarises the whole drama of our lives, the constant striving to transform personal sufferings and disappointments into a life-bringing crucifixion and burial with Christ. To help us in this participation, in Holy Week and Easter we follow through the Lord's Passover according to a historical time scale. This does, not, of course, mean that we take part in a historical exercise, requiring an effort of imagination to transport us mentally to first-century Palestine.

Historical description is not the goal of our search and our liturgical ascent. It is the gate through which we pass so as to enter, as far as is possible for us, into the unapproachable, secret actions of divine love, and the triumphant despoiling of sin and death.[12]

It is an intricate and elaborate process whereby the Paschal cycle guides the believer, through the familiar experience of linear time, to participate in Christ's passover. Within this cycle, lasting from three weeks before Lent to one week after Pentecost, there are three distinct unities, each different in character: (1) Lent and the weeks preceding it, (2) Holy Week, (3) Easter to Pentecost.

1 The inner coherence of Lent is not historical but ethical; it is characterised by a particular attitude and orientation. This is the time given to us to 'purify our senses' so as to 'see Christ shining like lightning in the unapproachable light of the resurrection'.[13] Even the weeks of preparation for Lent have a certain penitential character: the Sundays are dedicated successively to the Publican and the Pharisee, the Prodigal Son and the Last Judgement. Matins includes the Psalm of exile, Psalm 136/137, 'By the waters of Babylon we sat down and wept . . .', and special verses on Psalm 50/51. 'Open unto me the gates of repentance, O giver of life; for early in the morning my spirit seeks thy holy temple, bearing the temple of my body all defiled . . .'

Estrangement from God through sin, and return to him through repentance, through recognition of our fallenness, are the constant themes of the Lenten period. The last Sunday before Lent is the commemoration of Adam's expulsion from paradise 'because of eating' – because of taking food in disobedience. In this light, the Lenten fast, which precludes all animal products, represents a reintegration of our physical life into harmony with God's will – not, by any means, because God denies us the other good things of this world, but because in this way eating ceases to be an act of arbitrary individual choice.

The instinctive need for food, the greed for the individual's independent self-preservation, is transfigured in the context of the Church's fasting; submission to the common practice of the Church becomes paramount, turning eating into an act of relationship and communion.[14]

It is important in this context that the feasts should be taken just as seriously as the fasts as part of the Church's ascetic way.

The Sundays of Lent are still marked out as feasts, when wine and oil are taken; but even amidst the deeply penitential and very personal prayers of the weekday services, the resurrection is never lost from sight. The orientation and purpose of our Lenten journey is summed up in the final prayer of the plain and sombre Presanctified Liturgy, celebrated after Vespers on Wednesday and Friday, which asks, 'to accomplish the course of the fast, to keep inviolate the faith, to crush underfoot the heads of invisible serpents, to be accounted victors over sin, and uncondemned *to attain to and adore thy holy resurrection.*' In much the same way, the last words sung as Lent begins are those of the Easter troparion, 'Christ is risen from the dead, trampling down death by death, and to those in the tomb he has given life.'[15]

The service which culminates in the Presanctified Liturgy also contains another, less explicit pointer to Easter: the Kontakion of the Transfiguration:[16]

Thou wast transfigured on the mountain, and thy disciples beheld thy glory, O Christ God, as they were able; that, when they saw thee crucified, they might understand that thy suffering was voluntary, and might declare to the world that thou art truly the radiance of the Father.

Seeing the Transfiguration, we know that soon Christ will go up, not simply to a death, but to the 'exodus' which he is to accomplish at Jerusalem (cf. Luke 9.31).

In the middle of the Lenten fast, the Church reaches an oasis: it is the Veneration of the Cross. This, again, explores the mystery of the crucifixion – the death, not merely of a righteous man who gives his life for others, but of death itself. The Kontakion of this feast is a note of triumph, a message of salvation:

The fiery sword no longer guards the gate of Eden; for in a strange and glorious way, the wood of the cross has quenched its flame. The sting of death and the victory of sin are now destroyed, for thou hast come, my Saviour, crying to those in hell: return again to paradise.

It is, in short, an intimation of the resurrection; for, as St Gregory of Nyssa says:

What the grace of the resurrection promises us is nothing other than the restoration of those who were fallen of old. . . bringing back into paradise mankind, which had been expelled from it.[17]

The unbreakable nexus of cross and resurrection is proclaimed here, in the midst of Lent, in the verse sung solemnly as the cross is brought out in procession at the end of Matins, and used throughout the following week. 'Thy cross we venerate, O Master; and thy holy resurrection we glorify.' There is one even more striking, more daring sign of the paradoxical character of this feast. The *eirmoi* for the Kanon of the Cross, the first verse of each Ode, begin, 'The day of resurrection: let us be radiant, O peoples . . .' – they are the *eirmoi* of Easter.[18]

This 'ethical unity' of Lent effectively ends on the Friday before Palm Sunday. On the threshold of Holy Week, we encounter, not a foreshadowing of the passion, but the resurrection.

Giving us assurance of the general resurrection before thy passion, thou hast raised Lazarus from the dead, O Christ God. Therefore, like the children, we also carry tokens of victory, and cry to thee, the conqueror of death, Hosanna . . .(Troparion, Lazarus Saturday).

The Saturday of the Raising of Lazarus is thus a revelation of Christ's purpose when he leaves Bethany and goes up to Jerusalem to his passion, and of his life-giving power, which will be fresh in the mind of the worshipper as he contemplates Christ's death later in Holy Week. Lazarus Saturday is unique in that, liturgically, it is virtually a Sunday: it has most of the features otherwise reserved for the feast of the resurrection. This even extends to the singing of 'Now that we have seen Christ's resurrection', as after the Sunday Matins gospel. This apparently small detail is in fact of immense significance. We can make such a confession because we have seen the works of him who said to Martha, 'I am the resurrection and the life' (John 11.25).

There is a very close and ancient connection between Lazarus Saturday and Palm Sunday, as the above troparion – belonging to both feasts – suggests. The events of the Saturday throw light on those of the Sunday. 'Now that we have seen Christ's resurrection' in the raising of his friend, we are privileged with a new insight into the meaning of his triumphal entry into Jerusalem. He does indeed come as the king who will fight and emerge victorious, but his will be a struggle, and a triumph, not of national but of cosmic dimensions.

Seated in heaven upon thy throne, and on earth upon a foal, O Christ our God, thou hast accepted the praise of the angels and the songs of the children who cried out to thee: *Blessed art thou that comest to call back Adam* (Kontakion).

On Palm Sunday, there is no question of ignoring the coming passion; but it is awaited without terror, in full knowledge of Christ's purpose and his power. 'Let the people be renewed through sprinkling with the blood of God!' (Kanon). One of its most ancient hymns sets the tone for the Church's entry into Holy Week.

Today the grace of the Holy Spirit has brought us together, and we all take up thy cross and say: Blessed is he that cometh in the name of the Lord . . .

2 The historical continuity which characterises Holy Week is less prominent from Monday to Wednesday, but from Holy

Thursday onwards it is obviously crucial. In the Holy Thursday services, including the 'Twelve Gospels of the Passion' in the evening, the emphasis falls on the terrible deed committed by man against his God and Saviour, 'O mighty wonder! The creator of the world is delivered into the hands of lawless men . . .'[19] It is rather from Holy Friday that the tone of the services changes. I recall a monk from the Holy Mountain of Athos in Greece describing the Athonite Holy Week. 'You go into church on Great Friday, on Great Saturday, and you say, "Easter!" The festive vestments, the singing . . .' This is not accidental, it is not a partial anticipation of the feast of Easter: it is profoundly liturgical. Its meaning becomes clear if we underline the real disjunction and reorientation between Lent and Holy Week.

During the Lenten period . . . we never weep for the 'loss', the death of our Lord . . . for the Light which was extinguished on the cross . . . What makes us lament and experience unbearable pain is our own sins, the corruption of our human nature . . .
. . . This is why, as we approach the passion, the tone of our prayers becomes even more triumphant.[20]

To recall Christ's own passion with inconsolable grief, as if we thought his life was ended, would be mere historical make-believe; and our liturgical presence at an event which is historically past is at the opposite pole from make-believe of any kind.

When the Lord underwent his saving passion for the sake of the human race, the holy choir of apostles fell into great despondency, because they did not fully understand the outcome of the passion. But once they came to know the salvation that blossomed from it, then they named the proclamation of the passion 'good news'.[21]

We know the outcome of the passion; so once we turn from our own deadness to focus on the life-giving death of Christ, we cannot hide the fact that the passover has begun. There can be no single moment of time separating the two events, 'because it was not possible for the author of life to be held fast in corruption'.[22]

It is in this conscious certainty of the resurrection that the Church enters upon the great three days. At Vespers on Great Friday afternoon, the figure of Christ is taken down from the cross in the centre of the church just as this moment is being described in the gospel reading. The hymns speak of the awesome wonder of his death. And at the end of the service, the icon of the deposition is brought out of the altar in procession through the kneeling crowd, and placed on a decorated bier in front of the cross. Two troparia are sung: one speaks of Joseph of Arimathaea taking Christ's body from the cross, while the other looks forward.

The angel stood by the tomb, and to the women bearing spices he cried aloud: myrrh is fitting for the dead, but *Christ has shown himself a stranger to corruption*.

Christ as a stranger to corruption, the impossibility of the death and burial of God – this is felt with increasing intensity until the moment when we see him 'coming forth from the grave like a bridegroom' (Easter Kanon). On Friday evening, a third troparion is added to those just mentioned – it is none other than one of the regular Sunday resurrection troparia.

Going down to death, O life immortal, thou hast slain hell with the dazzling light of thy divinity. And when thou didst raise up the dead from their dwelling place beneath the earth, all the powers of heaven cried aloud: Giver of Life, Christ our God, glory to thee.

It is perhaps on this evening that the dynamic interpenetration of Christ's death and resurrection is most vividly illustrated. One of the most popular parts of the service is the 'Praises', sung to a majestic and triumphant melody while celebrants and people stand around the *epitaphion*, the decorated bier of Christ, holding candles. The 'Praises' are a long series of verses taking the form of a lament for Christ; they are of very late composition, and exhibit many of the features of medieval Greek folk lament. A few extracts will illustrate their character:

O life, how canst thou die? How canst thou dwell in a tomb? Yet thou dost destroy death's kingdom and raise the dead from hell.

Buried in the earth like a grain of wheat, thou hast yielded a rich harvest, raising to life the mortal sons of Adam.

Every generation, O my Christ, offers praises at thy burial.

'O my sweet springtime, O my sweetest child, where has all thy beauty gone?'

'Weep not, O Mother, for I suffer this to set at liberty Adam and Eve.'

By thy resurrection, give peace to thy Church and salvation to thy people.

It is with a gathering sense of anticipation, even excitement, that the Church awaits the resurrection as it celebrates 'the blessed Sabbath, the day of rest on which the Son of God rested from all his works'.[23] There is no doubt as to what is taking place on the cosmic plane during this time when we keep vigil before the bier of Christ as if it were one of his creatures whose coffin was lying in the church. At the end of the Great Saturday Kanon, Christ speaks.

'Let the creation rejoice exceedingly, let all those born on earth be glad: for hell, the enemy, has been despoiled. Ye women, come to meet me with sweet spices: for *I am delivering Adam and Eve with all their offspring*, and on the third day I shall rise again.'

Christ is given a funeral procession during the Friday evening service. It is a strange mystery: at this funeral, when the choir sings the processional prayer 'Holy God, Holy Mighty, Holy Immortal, have mercy on us', it is addressing the same Holy Immortal One whose body is carried out for burial, the Holy Mighty One whose might is revealed in his death. This extraordinary paradox is underlined through the remainder of the service. The concluding gospel ends with Christ's body in the tomb, guarded by a watch: but the Psalm verses preceding it tell a radically different story: 'Arise, O Lord my God, and let thy hand be lifted up: forget not thy poor for ever!' (Psalm 9/10.12) and 'Let God arise, and let His enemies be scattered (Psalm 167/168.2), with other verses otherwise used only for Easter.

3   There is no liturgical moment of the resurrection. Just as the authentic icon of the resurrection represents Christ, not leaping from the tomb, but trampling on death and hell, so the moment of his rising remains for ever mysterious; we know only that he was dead and is risen, raising up mankind with himself. Greek tradition gives the name of 'first resurrection' to a moment in Vespers and the Liturgy on Saturday morning. Instead of the normal Alleluia, the Epistle is followed by Psalm verses with the refrain, 'Arise, O God, judge thou the earth: for thou shalt have an inheritance in all the nations' (Psalm 81/82.8). At this moment, the church is transformed: the dark vestments and dark coverings are changed to white.

On Easter night itself, the resurrection of Christ is not announced even with the words 'Christ is risen!' – that comes later. In some fashion or other, we have accomplished the Lenten journey, we have been granted to come through the passion to the resurrection. We know the resurrection as the reality which has sustained us through the fast, up to this moment. It is not Christ but we who have returned once again from the dead, who through repentence dare once again to join in the eternal hymn of triumph. In a totally dark church, the celebrant, lighted candle in hand, processes around the altar as he sings, very quietly at first, 'Of thy resurrection, Christ our Saviour, the angels sing in heaven: grant also to us on earth with a pure heart to glorify thee.' And the royal doors are opened, the hymn grows louder, until the choir takes it up, and the light spreads from candle to candle to fill the whole church, 'Holy and all-festive indeed is this night of salvation, radiant with light – herald of the shining day of the resurrection, on which the timeless light shone forth upon all from the tomb' (Easter Kanon).

We shall not find any explicit theology of the resurrection on Easter night, and even very little typology of the passover: the intensity and immediacy of the experience is too dazzlingly bright. Nothing can be more fitting than the simple and incessantly-repeated affirmation which is the ground of the Church's faith, 'Christ is risen from the dead, trampling down death by death, and to those in the tombs he has given life.' When the encounter with the resurrection goes beyond words, we speak instead of the joy of the feast:

The day of resurrection! Let us be filled with radiance in this feast, let us embrace one another. Let us say, brethren, and to them that hate us, let us forgive all in the resurrection . . .

When on the evening of Holy Friday we heard the Psalm verses of Easter, they stopped short of the end. Now we hear them filling the air, and going on to the last verse, 'This is the day that the Lord has made – let us rejoice and be glad in it!' (Psalm 117/118.24) This day, the eighth day, the endless day of the Kingdom, is where we live, liturgically, from Easter to Pentecost. This whole period is an image of the resurrection, when there is no kneeling in church, and every day is liturgically a Sunday. This is most evident in the week following Easter, the 'week of renewal' or 'bright week'; there is no fasting at all, and the texts for each day are the Sunday texts in one of the eight Tones. We are living eternity within time.

'Today salvation has come to the world; let us sing to him who is risen from the dead,' says a troparion at the end of Sunday Matins. Both the prolonged experience of the resurrection during Pentecost and the weekly experience of Sunday constantly train our awareness so that we perceive the ever-present reality of the resurrection and live it. If we do not actually know that Christ is risen, if this is not the fundamental truth which informs all our perceptions, how can we live free from death: how can we proclaim the joy of salvation?

★ ★ ★

Liturgical life, life in the body of the risen Christ, is not a part of the Christian's experience: it defines the shape and illuminates the meaning of his total experience. Since his whole life is a drama of death and resurrection, there is a constant interpenetration between our everyday experience and the liturgical cycle. It is not accidental that so many of our examples of the resurrection in liturgical life have been taken from Holy Week. The 'externals' of the events represented here – betrayal, cruelty, ingratitude, faithlessness – loom large in our experience of the world and of ourselves, and it is this experience that we bring to the Church year by year. And we are taken through the externals to see their deeper meaning, the transformation worked by the presence of God incarnate – to meet the resurrection and the life in the lowest parts of hell.

To be real, our experience of death and resurrection must be profoundly personal; but at the same time it is wholly ecclesial, wholly integrated into our liturgical life.

The salvation given by the cross is salvation through Christ alone . . . Perfection is not to be found in human virtues, but is hidden in the cross of Christ.[24]

We do not enter into the resurrection because we have earned it through our individual moral efforts, but because the King has invited us to the marriage feast (cf. Matthew 22.9ff).

Enter ye all into the joy of your Lord . . . let no one weep for his sins, for forgiveness has shone forth from the tomb.[25]

When, therefore, we go out in to the world in the light of the resurrection, it is in the sure knowledge that the destruction of hell, the transformation of death into a passover into life, does not rest with our own strength . . . giving ourselves over to the contest in his hands, saying to God, thou art mighty, Lord, and thine is the contest: fight and conquer in it, for our sakes.'[26]

Elizabeth Briere is Russian Orthodox. Since 1983 she has been one of the Secretaries of the Fellowship of St Alban and St Sergius.

The resurrection in some modern novels

Richard Harries

IN IRIS MURDOCH'S NOVEL *The Good Apprentice* one of the characters is asked his view of Christ. He replies:

I have to think of him in a certain way, not resurrected, as it were mistaken, disappointed - well, who knows what he thought. He has to mean pure affliction, utter loss, innocent suffering, pointless suffering, the deep and awful and irremediable things that happen to people.[1]

This view, which reflects Iris Murdoch's own position in her philosophical essay *The Sovereignty of Good*[2] and which is derived from a particular reading of Simone Weil, presents a moral challenge to theologians that is too little considered. It may be put in this way. How can the resurrection of Christ be so affirmed that it can be clearly seen to be *morally* congruous with our deepest feelings about suffering? Like the character in Iris Murdoch's novel most people can see the moral appeal of a Christ who shares in the worst affliction of humankind. But how can his triumph over suffering be presented in a way that is sensitive to people experiencing 'the deep and awful and irremediable things'? Or so that it does not take away from the profound effect of a Christ who shares our bitter anguish? I suspect that underlying many of the radical interpretations of the resurrection of Christ there lies this question. For if the resurrection is understood simply as a matter of 'seeing' the suffering love of the cross to be triumphant, this has great moral appeal.[3] The affliction, Christ's and ours, is in no way diminished. It is simply understood in a different way, as a moral victory. The problem is how to state a more traditional view of the resurrection in such a way that it can be assented to on moral grounds (as well as historical ones) and which does not come across as a happy ending brought about by a *Deus ex machina*. Historical questions cannot be ignored and they must be answered honestly. But too often unrecognised assumptions and presuppositions push the scholar in a particular direction. There are assumptions about what is or is not possible. There are also assumptions about what is morally of a piece with our deepest insights about human suffering. It is best if these assumptions are taken out and examined. In particular it is important to see whether a traditional view of the resurrection can be stated in a way that is morally sensitive. If this is so, then there may be less unconscious pressure to look to a radical interpretation. It is therefore worth looking at the work of some novelists who have incorporated the resurrection into their work, to see how they have considered the matter. There is a particular kind of moral sensibility that makes for a great novelist, an imaginative sympathy, a sensitivity to the most delicate nuances of human feeling. At the least we can say that if a good novelist cannot write about the resurrection in such a way that carries moral conviction, no one can.

There is also another problem. The gospels depict a risen Christ able to come and go as he wills. He is not simply a resuscitated corpse like Lazarus but nor on the other hand is he only a vision in the minds of his followers. Depicting this on the stage is obviously difficult; the imaginative novelist, however, is not limited by physical restraints. In the popular stage production *Godspell* Jesus was depicted as a clown. In contrast to the philosophers of the world with their portentous sayings and ponderous ways Jesus was all light and laughter. After his death the audience was invited onto the stage and the bread of the last supper was shared round. All partook and the singing and clapping went on. This was a neat way of meeting two difficulties. There was no physical resurrection to be shown. The resurrection was the spirit of Jesus living again in the audience as they took the bread and were caught up in his *élan* and *joie de vivre*. Presenting the resurrection in this way also solved the problem of how to make the resurrection morally congruous with the crucifixion. Life, death and resurrection were of a piece, in the same style. But suppose we wish to depict, like the gospel writers, a raised and glorified body? And suppose we wish to do this without in any way cheapening the reality of Christ's affliction or ours? One way would be to look to the novelists. Encouragingly, and perhaps somewhat surprisingly, a number of major modern novelists have, in their various ways, dealt with these questions. I propose to consider three themes. First, the conviction of a redemptive power at work in the world; a power intimately connected with the historical Jesus. Secondly, the belief that this power is released into the world by a Christ-like death and thirdly, an exploration of how this redemptive power is related to an author's whole understanding of human life.

★   ★   ★

First, the conviction of a redemptive power at work in the world, a power intimately connected with the historical Jesus. I begin with Tolstoy's novel called *Resurrection* whose publication in serial form began in 1899. The plot can be simply told. A young aristocrat Nekhlúdoff seduces a peasant girl, Katisha Máslova. As a result she conceives, is thrown out of her employment and becomes a prostitute. Then, as a result of a false charge being brought against her, she is put into prison. There, some years after the seduction, Nekhlúdoff sees and recognises her. He is overcome with remorse, tries to obtain her release and fails. When she is sentenced he follows her to Siberia. The book is a massive indictment of Russian society at the time, particularly its judiciary and prison service. It is also about Nekhlúdoff's and Máslova's rebirth to a different kind of life. Inevitably the understanding of this life reflects Tolstoy's personal and social preoccupations. There is a strong contrast between the flesh and the spirit, in an un-Pauline sense, so that resurrection means overcoming sexual desire, regarded as evil. More centrally it meant that men should always acknowledge that they were sinning and, as a result of this, should refuse to condemn anyone else. Criminals should not be sentenced but forgiven and released. At the end of the novel Nekhlúdoff is given a New

Testament. He reads it all through the night, and he is overcome with the thought that the Sermon on the Mount could be literally put into practice.

He did not sleep all night, and as it happens to many and many a man who reads the Gospels, he understood for the first time the full meaning of the words read so often before but passed by unnoticed. He drank in all these necessary, important, and joyful revelations as a sponge imbibes water. . . The Master's will is expressed in these commandments. If men will only fulfil these laws the kingdom of heaven will be established on earth, and men will receive the greatest good that they can attain.

'And so here it is, the business of my life. Scarcely have I finished one, and another has commenced'. And a perfectly new life dawned that night for Nekhlúdoff, not because he had entered into new conditions of life, but because everything he did after that night had a new and quite different significance.[4]

I begin with Tolstoy's *Resurrection* primarily because it provides a contrast with a better, profounder novel written earlier by Dostoevsky. Dostoevsky's *Crime and Punishment* whose first instalments, appeared in 1866, and on some of whose themes one suspects that Tolstoy drew, brings out rather better than Tolstoy's novel the idea of a redemptive *power* at work.

Raskolnikov, the main character in *Crime and Punishment* is a strange perverse creature who longs to be a Napoleon figure, beyond good and evil. For no reason at all he murders two old ladies. Eventually his feelings of guilt lead him to admit the crime but not before he has met Sonia, who befriends him. The turning point for Raskolnikov is when Sonia reads to him the story of the raising of Lazarus. Then, in Siberia, where Sonia has followed him, he too reads the New Testament, indeed it was the same copy in which Sonia had read to him the story of the raising of Lazarus, and he wonders if her convictions can be his. The novel ends suggesting that as a result of this possibility there is a new story ahead, 'the story of the gradual regeneration of a man, the story of his gradual passing from one world to another, of his acquaintance with a new and hitherto unknown reality.'[5]

There are two immediate contrasts to be made with Tolstoy's treatment of the same theme. First, there is more emphasis in Dostoevsky on the existence of a transcendent order into which

Raskolnikov has been reborn. Secondly, his regeneration is brought about not only by the New Testament but by the power of Christian love working through Sonia. Sonia has been reduced to prostitution by the poverty of her family. But, in all her degradation and humiliation, she is kept going by her faith. It is the risen Christ working through her faith, her love and her prayers, that is the main instrument of Raskolnikov's regeneration. The main contrast, however, that I want to draw attention to is the fact that in Tolstoy's *Resurrection* it is obedience to the tenets of the Sermon on the Mount that is decisive, in *Crime and Punishment* it is resurrection grace and power breaking through the Lazarus story that is crucial. The whole scene is most tense and dramatic, though there is only space to quote a few words. Raskolnikov is urging her to read:

'Come on, read! I want you to!' he insisted. 'You used to read to Lisaveta, didn't you?'

Sonia opened the book and found the place. Her hands trembled, her voice failed her. Twice she tried to read without being able to utter the first syllable.

' "Now a certain man was sick, named Lazarus, of Bethany . . ." ,' she forced herself to say at last, but, suddenly, at the third word her voice rang and snapped like a string that had been screwed up too tightly.[6]

Raskolnikov knew that in reading Sonia was exposing her very heart, what was deepest and most precious for her:

But at the same time he knew now, and he knew it for certain, that, though she might feel upset and worried . . . she herself was most anxious to read to *him*, and to him alone, and to make sure that he *heard*, heard it *now*.

Eventually Sonia manages to continue reading:

' "Jesus said unto her, *I am the resurrection and the life*; he that believeth in me, though he were dead, yet shall he live: and whosoever liveth and believeth in me shall never die. Believest thou this? She saith unto him" ' (and as though drawing her breath painfully Sonia read slowly and distinctly the verse to the end, as though she were herself making a public confession of her faith): ' "Yea, Lord, I believe that thou art the Christ, the Son of God, which should come into the world." '

What is central to this novel is Christ as the resurrection and the life, working through the faith of Sonia, to raise Raskolnikov to new life.

In the end we cannot separate the moral claim of the gospel and the grace of the gospel. To know divine love is to know what love asks of us and to know what love asks of us is to know that it is love that asks. Furthermore, when the Church has averted its eyes so much from the claims of the Sermon on the Mount, it is right that prophetic figures like Tolstoy should direct us to them. But Dostoevsky's emphasis is truer both to life and the Christian life than that of Tolstoy. This may be reflected in the fact that Tolstoy himself was caught up in the most tragic and appalling contradictions and hypocrisies, whereas Dostoevsky achieved near sainthood. It may also be reflected in the fact that *Resurrection* is a much less satisfactory novel, with the Christian message tacked on at the end with little relationship to the story that has gone before. By contrast *Crime and Punishment* is a unity and its resurrection theme integral to the whole. In this novel the resurrection power of Christ, working through the faith and love of Sonia and communicated through the gospel story as she reads it, is the prior and fundamental reality. It is this resurrection power that makes it possible for Raskolnikov to discover and live in a new reality and begin to meet the ethical claims of that reality.

It is no accident that this emphasis on the resurrection power of Christ should be there in a Russian novel. For the resurrection is a present living reality for Orthodox thought in a way that it has never quite been for the Western Church. In the Western Church the stress has been on the death of Christ as the means of our redemption: in the Orthodox Church it is on the resurrection. I turn now to two more recent novels where the theme of resurrection is apparent, Patrick White's *Riders in the Chariot* and William Golding's *Darkness Visible*. Both are difficult novels, dense if not obscure in places. But in both there is a redemptive power let loose in the world as a result of a Christ-like death.

★　★　★

Riders in the Chariot is set in Australia. The climax of the novel comes when Himmelfarb, a Jewish refugee from Germany, is strung up in a mock crucifixion. The main theme of the book is the indivisibility of evil in the killing of Christ, Nazi Germany and Australian suburbia. Shortly after the mock crucifixion Himmelfarb dies. But his death is not the end. Strange things happen. But what things? Two ladies talking together after the events are at pains to emphasise there was no miracle. 'Only, there was no miracle. Definitely no miracle!'[7] Mrs Colquhoun was almost shouting. And there was indeed no miracle in the world of public events; or not that the readers can discern. But as a result of the death something happens to each of the four main characters. Each of the four has, throughout the novel, a mystic vision derived from the Book of Ezekiel, but for each of them their insight and way of life that ensues from it is very different. Miss Hare, who lives in a large, empty house, has a mystic communion with sticks and stones and animals. Alf Dubbo is a half-aboriginee who expresses his faith in paint. Mrs Godbold is a solid, kindhearted washerwoman. Himmelfarb himself is a practising Jew, who may be the expected Messiah. After his death, in which the other three are all involved in an inner, spiritual way, even though some of them are not physically present, they each in their different ways come to personal fulfilment. Alf Dubbo completes his painting then dies of T.B. Miss Hare has a mystic vision. Himmelfarb dies at peace. Mrs Godbold, a rock of love, continues to be a rock of love. Towards the end Mrs Godbold goes into church.

So, at last, the figure of her Lord and Saviour would stand before her in the chancel, looking down at her from beneath the yellow eyelids, along the strong, but gentle beak of a nose. She was content to leave then since all converged finally upon the Risen Christ, and her own eyes had confirmed that the wounds were healed.

That evening, as she walked along the road, it was the hour at which the other gold sank its furrows in the softer sky. The lids of her eyes, flickering beneath its glow, were gilded with the identical splendour. But, for all its weight, it lay lightly, lifted her, in fact, to where she remained an instant in the company of the living creatures she had known, and many others she had not. All was ratified again by hands.[8]

All the four main characters have a vision of a transcendent, spiritual realm. Each of them is on the edge of ordinary society, despised or disregarded by the pushers and thrusters. Each of them is mystically bound up with the death of Himmelfarb and the events following his death are conscious echoes of the crucifixion story. Another Jew, who has been involved in a kind of betrayal, commits suicide. Mrs Godbold, as she does her washing, remembers the deposition. What distinguishes the four is a failure in worldly terms that opens them up to receive the reality of the spiritual world, a failure brought to a climax at death. Himmelfarb, as he lies dying, thinks of his father, 'Always separate during the illusory life of men now they touched, it seemed, at the point of failure.'[9] Then he thought of his wife and what she stood for and had tried to convey to him.

It seemed to him as though the mystery of failure might be pierced only by those of extreme simplicity of soul, or else by one who was about to doff the outgrown garment of the body. He was weak enough, certainly, by now to make the attempt which demands the ultimate in strength.

This mystery of weakness, of failure, which comes to its appointed focus in death, is shared by the four riders in the divine chariot. The death of Himmelfarb, his extreme point of human failure, seems to allow the power of a transcended order to flood into the world and affect the lives of others living as he did, in such a way as to help bring them to their appointed spiritual fulfilment. Indeed for all of them in their different ways the words of Paul are true.

For his sake I have suffered the loss of all things, and count them as refuse. . . that I may know him and the power of his resurrection, and may share his sufferings, becoming like him in his death that if possible I may attain the resurrection from the dead.[10]

In our mundane way we ask what is the relationship between the death of Himmelfarb and what happens to the other three. The very denseness and difficulty of the writing, particularly in the last few chapters, suggests that there is no mundane answer. The suburban ladies raise the question of miracle but there is no miracle they can see and they are anxious to deny that there has been one. But for those other riders in the chariot, something has certainly happened: happened to them and in them and through them. Miss Hare has a vision of her friend Himmelfarb, 'She stood in the everlasting moment.' Alf Dubbo finishes off his picture of Christ, just before he himself dies.

Once on emerging from behind the barricades of planes, the curtain of textures, he ventured to retouch the wounds of the dead Christ with the love he had never dared express in life, and at once the blood was gushing from his own mouth, the wounds in the canvas were shining and palpitating with his own conviction.[12]

Mrs Godbold the rock of love, has her vision, but continues to serve on earth.

She would lower her eyes to avoid the dazzle, and walk on, breathing heavily, for it was a stiff pull up the hill, to the shed in which she continued to live.[13]

William Golding's *Darkness Visible* is the most ambitious of his novels and perhaps the most ambitious of all the books here considered. The central character is Matty, who emerges out of a fire in London's blitz most terribly disfigured. In hospital, adults 'hurrying to their own unfortunates, were repelled by the sordid misery in which Matty passed his days, and they flashed sideways at him an uneasy smile which he interpreted with absolute precision.'[14] At school he was terribly teased. At the ironmongers where for a time he had a job , 'He was perpetually employed and never knew that people gave him jobs to get him out of their sight.'[15] Matty's mind is a strange one, scarred as it is by his terrible experience but it formulates a pressing question 'Who am I?' The question is never answered but Matty comes to reformulate it, 'What am I for?' and to feel that he exists for something. In schemes reminiscent of the wandering of the people of Israel Matty pursues his way before becoming an odd job man in a private school. Then, in a terrorist attack on the school, he is accidentally blown up and killed. Matty seems to become one of the flames in the fire, fire being a key image in the book. The flames of fire cause one of the terrorists, fleeing with a child, to let go of the boy who then escapes. But even more remarkable is what happens next. Whilst a child Matty had met a Mr Pedigree, a pederast. Mr Pedigree was revolted by Matty but Matty, through some strange misreading of the relationship, became devoted to Mr Pedigree. Mr Pedigree is caught up in a cycle which from time to time leads him to attempt sexual relationships with a child. At the time of Matty's death Mr Pedigree is in the grip of one of his compulsive cycles and is waiting outside a public lavatory for some children. Matty appears to him in a vision of gold to free him from his enslavement.

He came slowly to Mr Pedigree who found his approach not only natural but even agreeable for the boy was not really as awful to look at as one might think, there where he waded along waist deep in gold. He came and stood before Pedigree and looked down at him. Pedigree understood that they were in a park of mutuality and closeness where the sunlight lay right on the skin.

'You know it was all your fault Matty.'

Matty seemed to agree; really the boy was quite pleasant to look at![16]

As in *Riders in the Chariot* there is a contrast between two worlds. When the terrorists attack the school in order to kidnap the children the media is focused upon all the outward events. TV cameras and newspaper men are caught up in what is happening. The death of an obscure, strange odd job man is not noticed. But while the world watches these dramatic outward happenings another plot is all the time being worked out. Matty is an agent of redemption. He knows his life exists for something and his death releases him from the constraints of time and space for the redemption of Mr Pedigree. Matty becomes at once a flame of fire and a vision of gold.

★　★　★

The third theme I want to explore is the relationship between an author's understanding of resurrection and their wider concerns. In addition to the novels already mentioned I refer in particular to D. H. Lawrence's story *The Man who Died* and R. C. Hutchinson's novel *Rising*. In contrast to his popular reputation D. H. Lawrence was a religious man who wrote some of the profoundest poetry on death of our time. He also had a relationship with the Christian faith, albeit an ambivalent one. He was at once attracted and repelled by Christian concepts of virtue. In *The Man who Died* a man, who is obviously meant to be Jesus, regains consciousness in the tomb, the crucifixion not having fully killed him. He emerges and after a period with a peasant family goes to live with a priestess, Isis. Jesus, in the story, comes to re-evaluate his ministry and reject it as based on death. Through the healing hands of the goddess he comes to a new life of tenderness and touch. The priestess starts to annoint and rub his wounds and as she does so brings him to real life. They begin to talk about the woman in the gospels who annointed him with oil and Jesus reflects.

I asked them all to serve me with the corpse of their love. And in the end I offered them only the corpse of my love. This is my body – take and eat – my corpse –

A vivid shame went through him. 'After all,' he thought, 'I wanted them to love with dead bodies. If I had kissed Judas with live love, perhaps he would never have kissed me with death.'

There dawned on him the reality of soft, warm love which is in touch and which is full of delight. . .

And he ıı. the recurring dismay of having died, and in the anguished perplexity of having tried to force life, felt his wounds crying aloud, and the deep places of the body howling again: 'I have been murdered, and I lent myself to murder. They murdered me, but I lent myself to murder.'[17]

Jesus feels sexual desire arising in him, senses death going and life coming. Afterwards 'in the absolute stillness and fullness of touch, he slept in the cave'[18] at one with the woman, the world and himself.

The story reflects a number of Lawrence's personal preoccupations, not least his own disillusionment with the role of prophet. He came to see, and therefore made Jesus see, that you cannot impose a new order on things. The value of *The Man who Died* from the standpoint of Christian theology is twofold. First, it forces Christians to think about celibacy and the prophetic role, in particular the prophetic role of Jesus in bringing in the Kingdom of God, and it makes us seek ways of talking about these things which are not open to Lawrence's strictures that they are simply disguised forms of death. Secondly, although we would want, on historical grounds, to reject Lawrence's reconstruction of the course of events, his theme can be affirmed as an aspect of or effect of Christian redemption. For Christianity, which believes that creation was made good; that God took flesh and dwelt among us; which believes in the resurrection of the body, is not stand-offish about the body. To live consciously and joyously as a physical being, as a body, not simply in its sexual aspects but in all its physicality, is part of redemption. There is a temptation to say that if what Lawrence describes has a place in the Christian understanding of resurrection, it must be as the fruit of a prior spiritual transformation. But it is wiser to heed the words of Edwin Muir.

> Whether the soul at first
> This pilgrimage began,
> Or the shy body leading
> Conducted soul to soul
> Who knows? This is the most
> That soul and body can,
> To make us each for each
> And in our spirit whole.[19]

Lawrence's approach to the resurrection story brings out starkly how its interpretation is related to our whole understanding of life. This is true of all writers. One value of Lawrence is that he throws into relief some more traditional interpretations and shows them as also making claims, if of a rather different kind. In R. C. Hutchinson's novel *Rising* Sabino, a member of a leading South American family, is sent with a private army to guard part of a railway line that is being attacked by guerrillas. Earlier in his life Sabino had sentenced a man from this area to be brutally tortured to death. Now he finds himself, with a broken leg, captured by a member of that man's family. He is expecting a similar long drawn out death. But a strange experience happens to him. An Indian surgeon comes to him and through the touch of his hands heals his leg. They talk about the nature of healing and the surgeon says it is necessary for Sabino to yield to affection, to yield to the healer who cares for him. They begin to talk about the man whom many years before Sabino had killed, or thought he had killed. Sabino looks at the man before him and sees that same man of many years before. Is it a dream or is it real?[20] Certainly his leg is healed. Sabino comes back to his family. Unfortunately, R. C. Hutchinson died as he was finishing the novel but he left notes on how he intended to go on. Sabino is to realise, hard man that he is, the supremacy of love, of Christian love.

Only when he has realised that if . . . he puts himself into the hands of the risen Christ as his follower, he may do wrong again, he may even be proud and cruel again, but never again will he be without the knowledge that, in his new life, he can be forgiven and can find peace.[21]

Another note added, 'We want, finally, a sense of things not ending but freshly beginning.'

This novel makes clear what was perhaps more movingly explored in Hutchinson's novel *Johanna at Daybreak*[22], that redemption is fundamentally a moral matter, it is redemption of sinners. Sabino is a hard man who has tried to put at least one person cruelly to death. In *Johanna at Daybreak* the central character is a woman who has handed her husband and children over to the Nazis and who has to come, through divine judgement and divine forgiveness, to live with the fact. In *Rising* this redemption is initiated by the dream or reality of the person Sabino has tried to kill offering affection and healing. The *Rising* of the title has a threefold reference, to peasant risings, the rising from death, or apparent death, of the person Sabino sent to a cruel death and the rising to new life of Sabino himself. In this emphasis on moral redemption Hutchinson stands with Golding and Dostoevsky. This does not mean to say that the understanding of Patrick White and D.H.Lawrence is valueless. Far from it. White brings out the fact that redemption involves individual vocation, Lawrence the point that it should include an affirmation of and oneness with the physical. Yet both these are in fact manifestations of a redemption which is first of all moral redemption, for redemption, whichever way it is looked at, must have choice at its core and therefore also contrition, forgiveness and transformation by grace.

★　★　★

I began by suggesting that there were two problems that anyone who wishes to discuss the resurrection of Christ in traditional terms is faced with. First, if the resurrection cannot be neatly categorised as either physical or visionary, how can it be depicted in a way which carries conviction? Novelists, whose work is not bound by physical restraints and who can make use of the boundless power of the imagination, are here in a good position. What is noteworthy about the treatments considered is that they leave the sense of mystery about what exactly happened at the resurrection intact. The good ladies of the Australian suburbs want to talk about miracle and yet insist that no miracle has happened. That something has happened we are left in no doubt, but exactly *what* is known differently to the people to whom it has happened and known by them at their points of deepest conviction. Even in *Darkness Visible,* which comes closest to a visible manifestation, the blown-up Matty takes shape both as a rescuing flame and as a vision to Mr Pedigree. In both these novels, however, what happens after the death of the Christ figure is not just a change in outlook in a few people. Something is released into the world by the death; a presence, a power, a person. In Dostoevsky the emphasis is different from that of White and Golding because he is not dealing with the resurrection as an event in history but with resurrection power as a present reality. In *Crime and Punishment* we see this reality,working through the faith and love of Sonia and becoming recognisable as such through the words of scripture. Here the God who raised Christ Jesus from the dead, and who will raise us from death into immortal life, is experienced now raising us from the death of sin and despair. The same is true in Hutchinson's *Rising* where it seems to be deliberately unclear whether the man whom Sabino sent to his death is in fact physically alive, having survived death, or a vision of a risen presence. In either case it is a loving, healing, redeeming power personified that is at work. In none of these novels do the authors fail to convince, except in the case of Tolstoy, whose view anyway can be questioned on theological grounds. This is not, of course, in any sense proof that the resurrection of Christ happened, only that it can be presented by accomplished novelists in such a way that those who read the books experience the same degree of reality when resurrection is being described as when mundane facts are written about. The level of conviction does not falter when we move from crucifixion, which we know can happen, to resurrection.

The second problem concerned the moral congruity of the resurrection with our deepest insights about human suffering. How can we speak of it in a way that does not belittle the affliction of human beings, that does not appear morally cheap?

It is easier to write a novel that deals only with the crucifixion.[23]
We can respond to a God who shares our loss and woe. In the
novels considered the resurrection of Christ is seen in intimate
connection to the divine redemptive purpose. It may be that in
recent years the resurrection of Christ has been seen too
exclusively against the background of the crucifixion and not in
this wider context. The earliest Christian preaching saw the
resurrection of Christ as the beginning of the general
resurrection. They preached not only that Christ was risen but
that he would soon return to judge the quick and the dead. In
early Christian art, particularly in its Eastern form, the
resurrection is most intimately connected with the harrowing of
hell. The great Byzantine mosaics and frescoes of the 10th and
11th century show Christ rising from the dead and at the same
time hauling Adam and Eve and the good men of old out of their
grave.[24] In the Medieval West the harrowing of hell was also a
major theme. For example, in the recent production of *The
Mysteries* a cycle of three mystery plays, it is the harrowing of
hell that is the major theme in the last one. The resurrection of
Christ occurs, but it is, as it were, an incident on the way to the
raising of all the dead. In the novels discussed here the prime
thrust of the action is the redemption of human souls. The risen
presence and power at work to this end is, as it were, the
incarnation carried on by other means. The resurrection of
Christ is the essential point of transition, enabling the work of
Christ to go on unconstrained by the limits of time and space.
This is not to deny that there are important historical questions
to answer, for Christianity makes a claim about what happened
in history. But when we are considering the moral significance
and appropriateness of the resurrection these novels suggest
that the resurrection has to be seen in a much wider context than
the crucifixion. If the resurrection is isolated from the wider
context it is easy to obtain the impression that it is simply a
reversal of the crucifixion. Within the wider context it can be
seen as an essential transition point in the carrying out of God's
redemptive purpose for all of human kind. There is another
point. If divine redemptive work is a concept to which one can
morally give assent then this calls into question some of the
presuppositions that Iris Murdoch, amongst others, brings to

bear. It forces one to ask whether there is not a victim mentality, a defeatist pathology that is influencing the whole way some people look at what is or is not morally appropriate. For a Christ who is all loss, all affliction, is morally appropriate to an age which can see nothing but loss and affliction. But the Christian faith has always been preached as good news about the ultimate triumph of divine love. An age which cannot conceive of the possibility of anything but tragedy will, understandably enough, have difficulty in grasping the moral appropriateness of the resurrection. Nevertheless that resurrection (as witnessed to by the novels discussed) calls into question the very assumptions by which we judge what is and what is not morally proper.

The novels considered here illuminate the resurrection of Christ in at least four ways.

(1) They show that it is possible to write about the resurrection in a way that carries literary conviction. There is no unnatural break between the suffering and the triumph. All novel reading involves a suspension of disbelief. But no greater, or different, suspension of disbelief is called for in writing about the resurrection than in writing about the crucifixion.

(2) They show that it is possible to write about the resurrection in a way that carries moral conviction, which does justice to our deepest feelings about human suffering.

(3) They understand the resurrection against the background of a divine redemptive purpose at work in the world. Except in the case of Lawrence, that is conceived of in fundamentally moral terms.

(4) They lead us to question the presuppositions that we bring to bear in judging what is or is not morally appropriate. The novels are concerned with the *achievement* of redemption, with the *accomplishment* of the divine purpose of love. They lead us to ask why it is that so many today are drawn to a defeated Christ but not a victorious, glorified one.

Richard Harries is bishop of Oxford.

Did Jesus really rise from the dead?

Eric Mascall

I

IT IS ONE OF THE IRONIES of recent scholarship that, just at the time when Dr David Jenkins was celebrating his nomination to the Bishopric of Durham by utterances which left his hearers in considerable doubt whether he believed in the resurrection of Jesus in any normally accepted or clearly assignable meaning of the phrase, a book appeared by a biblical scholar who is a practising Jew and who accepts the resurrection of Jesus in the most literal and realistic way. The reader of a small but concentrated work **The Resurrection of Jesus: A Jewish Perspective**[1] by Dr Pinchus Lapide will find in it none of the watering down, none of the 'readjustment' to the alleged needs of an anti-supernatural culture which was the leading motive of the weary symposium *The Myth of God Incarnate*.[2] There is no suggestion that the resurrection stories were the outcome of wishful thinking on the part of the disciples, who could not bear to think that Jesus was not still with them, or that they were skilfully adapted myths originating in the welter of rites and rituals of the Gentile world. On the contrary, Lapide maintains, the stories are Jewish to the core; and what they describe is the amazing reversal of an event happening within Judaism and to a group of Jews which, but for that reversal, must have remained what it originally had been, namely the most shattering catastrophe. 'The panic-stricken horror of the disciples which both Mark and Matthew describe as a headlong flight; either their master's death on the cross or the fact that at Golgotha a change of Jesus into the messianic Son of man did not take place could have instilled this clear feeling of failure in them.' But, in that case, asks Lapide:

How can it be explained that, against all plausibility, his adherents did *not* finally scatter, were *not* forgotten, and that the cause of Jesus did *not* reach its infamous end on the cross?. . .

In other words: How did it nevertheless come about that the adherents of Jesus were able to conquer this most horrible of all disappointments, that Jesus, despite everything, became the Saviour of the Church, although his predictions were not fulfilled and his longed-for parousia did not take place?

Lapide tells us that the answer of the apostles was brief and unambiguous: the resurrection of Jesus from the dead. And, although he is ready to admit that the resurrection is not open to public verification and indeed suggests that only a Jew can fully understand it, he insists upon its objective and historic character. He even makes use of the medieval Jewish scholar Maimonides to ask whether, in view of 'the pedagogy of God', 'Would it not be possible that the Lord of the universe used the myth of the resurrection (which was well known to all pagans) in order "to eliminate idolatry in the pagan world" through the true resurrection of a just person and to carry "the knowledge of God" to the four corners of the earth by means of the Easter faith?'[3]

In any case, he insists:

The resurrection of Jesus on that Easter Sunday and his appearance in the following days were purely Jewish faith experiences. Not one Gentile saw him after Good Friday. Everything that the Gentile church heard about the resurrection came only from Jewish sources because he appeared after Easter Sunday as the Risen One exclusively to Jews.[4]

And, he asserts, scientific analysis suggests three possibilities: (1) that the resurrection was a historical event that took place in this world in the first century in Jerusalem; (2) that it is a religious myth, as in the mystery cults of the ancient Orient; (3) that the reports rest on visions of individual persons who experienced them as real experiences but so as to be completely inaccessible to the objective tests of the sciences. His own view he insists on describing in essentially Jewish terms:

In regard to the future resurrection of the dead, I am and remain a Pharisee. Concerning the resurrection of Jesus on Easter Sunday, I was for decades a Sadducee. I am no longer a Sadducee since the following deliberation has caused me to think this through anew. In none of the cases where rabbinic literature speaks of such visions did it result in an essential change in the life of the resuscitated or of those who had experienced the visions . . .

It is different with the disciples of Jesus on that Easter Sunday. Despite all the legendary embellishments, in the oldest records there remains a recognisable historical kernel which cannot simply be demythologised. When this scared, frightened band of the apostles which was just about to throw away everything in order to flee in despair to Galilee; when these peasants, shepherds, and fishermen, who betrayed and denied their master and then failed him miserably, suddenly could be changed overnight into a confident mission society, convinced of salvation and able to work with much more success after Easter than before Easter, then no vision or hallucination is sufficient to explain such a revolutionary transformation.[5]

Lapide is not easy to satisfy. 'I cannot believe,' he writes, without saying why, 'in the empty tomb nor in the angels in white garments nor in the opening of the heaven nor in the absurd miraculousness of the so-called Gospel of Peter.'[6] Yet, he rejects as unsatisfactory the 'strange paraphrases', as he calls them, which modern theologians frequently use for the resurrection of Jesus, and gives no less than six examples of these; 'they strike me,' he writes, 'as all too abstract and scholarly to explain the fact that the solid hillbillies from Galilee . . . were changed within a short period of time into a jubilant community of believers.'[7] And he offers a rebuke which is all the more impressive for coming, as it does, from a man who does not believe in the incarnation:

I cannot rid myself of the impression that some modern Christian theologians are ashamed of the material facticity of the resurrection. Their varying attempts at dehistoricising the Easter experience which give the lie to all four evangelists are simply not understandable to me in any other way. Indeed, the four authors of the gospels definitely compete with one another in illustrating the tangible, susbstantial dimension of this resurrection explicitly. Often it seems as if renowned New Testament scholars in our days want to insert a kind of ideological or dogmatic curtain between the pre-Easter and the risen Jesus in order to protect the latter against any kind of contamination by earthly three-dimensionality. However, for the first Christians who thought, believed and hoped in a Jewish manner, the immediate historicity was not only a part of that happening but the indispensable precondition for the recognition of its significance for salvation. For all these Christians who believe in the incarnation (something which I am unable to do) but have difficulty with the historically understood resurrection, the word of Jesus of the 'blind guides, straining out a gnat and swallowing a camel' (Matthew 25.4) probably applies.[8]

At this point a Christian can hardly help asking how it is that Lapide, believing as he does in the resurrection of Jesus as both a historical and a supernatural event, can fail to take the step of becoming a Christian himself. The answer is that, although he believes in the resurrection of Jesus, he does not believe that Jesus is the Messiah, the Christ, the Anointed of God. 'Jesus,' he writes, 'without doubt, belongs to the *praeparatio messianica* of the full salvation which is still in the future. He was a "paver of the way for the King Messiah", as Maimonides calls him, but this does not mean that his resurrection makes him the Messiah of Israel for Jewish people.' Lapide quotes from a Catholic theologian Clemens Thoma:

For Jewish scholars, the testimony of the resurrection was no proof for the messiahship of Jesus because for them the concept of resurrection is not connected with the messianic expectation of salvation. At the time of Jesus, Judaism was expecting the resurrection of various figures: of Enoch, of Moses, of Elijah, of Jeremiah, . . but not the resurrection of the Messiah.[9]

Yet Lapide feels bound to admit that the explosion of missionary activity which resulted from a handful of Jews being convinced that the risen Jesus was in fact the Messiah was, in spite of their misunderstanding, a manifestation of the saving activity of God:

As a faithful Jew, I cannot explain a historical development which, despite many errors and much confusion, has carried the central message of Israel from Jerusalem into the world of the nations, as a result of blind happenstance, or human error, or a materialistic determinism – although all these factors possibly may have helped advance the divine plan of salvation. The experience of the resurrection as the foundation act of the church which has carried the faith in the God of Israel into the whole Western world must belong to God's plan of salvation.[10]

It is impossible not to be deeply moved by the way in which Judaism, throughout its tragic history, with its culmination in our own time in the horror of the Nazi holocaust, has preserved its faith in a Messiah who it believes has not yet come and its hope in a world which it believes is still unredeemed. Lapide writes:

Indeed, this world remains unsaved, and we all are still suffering in it just as we also are still responsible for it. But that experience of a handful of Bible-believing Jews who were able to carry their faith in God into the Gentile world must surely be interpreted as a God-willed encouragement in a world that so often seems hopeless.[11]

We Christians, to whom in God's mercy it has been revealed that the Jew Jesus who was raised from the dead is none other than the Messiah of God, and that in him the renewal and regeneration of the world is, in spite of all appearances, already taking place, should feel both humble and grateful before God's ancient people the Jews through whom this revelation has been made known to us and we have been brought to share in it. For any type of anti-semitism there can be no shadow of justification; Jesus was crucified by Jews and Gentiles alike and he was himself a Jew. Dr Lapide's book is a splendid contribution to that dialogue between Jews and Christians for which Vatican II urgently appealed. He admits very frankly that orthodox Christians believe more about Jesus than he, an orthodox Jew, is able to believe. But also – and this may well cause deep shame to Christians – it is plain from his discussion that, as an orthodox Jew, he finds himself able, and indeed forced, to believe much more about Jesus than Christians of the 'liberal' or 'radical' type would be prepared to admit. And this is indeed a refreshing and astringent conclusion to a brief but very significant book.

II

I turn now to another book about the resurrection, published at the same time as Dr Lapide's and of equal interest, but of a very different kind **Easter Enigma** by John Wenham.[12] Its background is the almost universal assumption which is made by writers about the New Testament today, that, whatever may be the precise character of the five accounts which we have of the resurrection of Jesus – those in the four Gospels and that given by St Paul in 1 Corinthians 15 – they cannot be, or at any rate most of them cannot be, reliable and straightforward pieces of reporting. And the reason given is that, as it is alleged, they simply do not agree with one another. About what they *are,* opinions vary wildly: some have alleged that they are borrowings from contemporary pagan mythology, some that they are the effects of candlelight upon highly suggestible temperaments, some that they are material elaborately worked up for preaching purposes, some would even claim to extract a structure of fact from the mass of fiction that has hidden it. Some are willing to accept the stories as beautiful and edifying legends and even to treat them as having valuable symbolic meanings as long as they are not alleged to be descriptions of actual happenings, while others treat them as relics of an outworn supernaturalism which modern men and women will rightly refuse to accept. But almost all agree – even Lapide, with a remark about 'secondary embellishments'[13], comes on occasion near to admitting this – that the stories cannot be accurate and straightforward accounts, *because they simply do not agree with one another.*

Now at first glance this objection seems very weighty, and Wenham illustrates it himself from the events of the first Easter morning. 'Luke mentions at least five women at the tomb, while Mark refers to three, Matthew to two, John to one and Paul to none at all. John puts the visit to the tomb while it was still dark and Mark when the sun had risen . . .'[14] But before you can validly assert that two accounts contradict each other, it is essential to make sure that they are describing precisely the same event, and moreover are describing it at the same moment and from the same point of view. In addition, there is always the possibility, especially when the event is a supernatural one, that it may appear in different ways to different observers. This, of course, may make the task of identification difficult, but it provides no justification for asserting contradiction where contradiction has not been shown to exist. And it must be admitted that many scholars who have written about the resurrection have shown little concern for this kind of exact precision. They have rather tended to take the variety of the stories as *prima facie* evidence of their unreliability. And even those who accept their broad witness to the resurrection are usually willing to concede their alleged inaccuracy in matters of detail, without making any detailed examination. One person who had, however, to make a detailed examination was the late Dorothy L. Sayers who, in the early nineteen-forties, had undertaken the formidable task, which gave little opportunity for ambiguities and evasions, of giving concrete expression to the gospel narratives in a series of plays on the radio. And here is her own description of her discovery:

The playwright. . . is often surprised to find how many apparent contradictions turn out not to be contradictory at all, but merely supplementary. Take, for example, the various accounts of the resurrection appearances at the sepulchre. The divergences appear very great on first sight; and much ink and acrimony have been expended on proving that certain of the stories are not 'original' or 'authentic', but are accretions grafted upon the first-hand reports by the pious imagination of Christians. Well, it may be so. But the fact remains that *all* of them, without exception, can be made to fall into place in a single orderly and coherent narrative without the smallest contradiction or difficulty, and without any suppression, invention, or manipulation, beyond a trifling effort to *imagine* the natural behaviour of a bunch of startled people running about in the dawnlight between Jerusalem and the Garden.[15]

It is, to my mind, astonishing, how little attention has been paid to Miss Sayers's evidence, and indeed how blind scholars have been to the opportunities offered by this method of correlating and assessing the gospel material. However, we must now turn to the work of John Wenham, and the first point to notice is that he had actually resided in Jerusalem and made a precise analysis of the various incidents in detail. He gave minute attention to all the minutiae of time, place and personal identity, and the results are recorded in a complete sequence of admirably lucid sketch-maps. These need to be followed step by step, and to do this is fascinating as an exercise in detection quite apart from its significance for Christian faith. Wenham writes:

I had no real doubts that the gospel writers were honest and well informed people, providentially equipped by God to give the church a sound account of these events, but I was by no means committed to the view that the accounts were correct in every detail. Indeed I was impressed in my early studies of the resurrection stories by the seemingly intractable nature of the discrepancies .

But an insatiable curiosity made me want to know who did what and why each writer put things so.[16]

And here is the result of his investigation:

The charge of irreconcilability brought against the resurrection stories has not been proved. Rather [the investigation] has shown that these records exhibit the characteristics of accurate and independent reporting, for superficially they show great disharmony, but on close examination the details gradually fall into place. We have seen how an accurate knowledge of topography, a full acquaintance with the actors in the drama and an understanding of the differing viewpoints of the narrators, all throw light on the probable course of events. Maybe there are problems not fully solved and problems given a wrong solution, but when every effort has been made to give the details of the narratives their full weight, they add up to a consistent story.

Wenham wisely adds the reminder that:

The imperfect knowledge that we have gained by laborious effort nearly two millennia after the events was of course immediately accessible in a fuller and more accurate form to those who had lived through them.

And so, he concludes:

The possession of such knowledge goes far towards explaining the certainty, stability and depth of the faith of the early Christians in their risen Lord.[17]

This does not mean that Wenham claims to settle every question that can possibly be raised. As he himself says, 'Many of the details are of course uncertain. Imagination and reasoned conjecture inevitably play a part in trying to picture things as they were.'[18] (On one particular issue - that of the 'brothers of Jesus' – he departs from the common Catholic view.[19]) But he is insistent that the different stories of the empty tomb and of the resurrection appearances are consistent, and he sees them not as mutually exclusive alternatives but as coherent contributions to an overall picture. Thus he writes:

The initial appearances in Jerusalem were clearly important evidentially. There was great psychological value in staying around within walking distance of the empty tomb for eight days, to preclude the possibility of any later suspicion of hallucination . . . but all this was preparatory to the great gathering in the hills of Galilee . . . In Galilee the apostles were made the instrument for regathering the scattered believers, and in their presence they were recommissioned. They were re-formed as the leaders of a great company who had become witnesses of the resurrection. In the atmosphere of Galilee they were weaned afresh from the idea of a temporal Jewish Messianic Kingdom, till ready to be sent back to the city which had crucified the Lord to begin their worldwide witness. . . There only remained the last farewell and the waiting for the Spirit's power, which would send them out to turn the world upside down.[20]

This is a vastly fuller and richer view of the resurrection and of the risen Lord than is allowed us by any of those outlooks which single out as admissible one particular aspect or element (usually one which is congenial to contemporary prejudices) and then reject all those that do not obviously fit in with it.

III

Finally, I want to raise the question whether, in the last resort, it really matters whether Jesus literally rose from the dead or not? What difference can it make to me or anyone else if the story of the resurrection is just a haunting story of something that never in fact occurred, expressing a nostalgic and tragic sense of the inevitable frustration of the noblest human ideals and aspirations? Or even if it witnesses to the survival and triumph of Jesus in a purely spiritual form, while his body was left to decay in the grave as rubbish of no further importance? The answer is that it matters enormously, for the following reasons.

First, that the incarnation – God becoming man – is not just an idea, a pleasant way for us to think about things, but was an actual intervention by God into the process of the universe, and this had its climax in the resurrection.

Secondly, in the incarnation God assumed human nature in its wholeness, body no less than soul, in order to restore it and regenerate it in its wholeness. Therefore Jesus's body, no less than his soul, was brought back to life, and not discarded, in his resurrection.

But, thirdly, in his resurrection Jesus's body is not just reanimated as a kind of zombie but is transformed and glorified, raised to a new level of being. Precisely what is involved in this transformation we are unable to say, but the glimpses that we have in the Gospels and in the Acts of the Apostles make two things clear: it was the *same* body which was crucified and laid in the grave, but it was in a totally new condition which overcame the normal limitations of material objects. This casts a great deal of light upon the essential nature and the ultimate destiny of the physical universe; it has long been an accepted principle of Catholic theology that grace does not destroy nature but perfects it; we can expand this in the form that grace neither destroys nor rejects nor ignores nature, but welcomes, needs, perfects and transforms it. And because there still appear to be people who, after nearly a century of relativity and quantum theory, think of the material world as composed of indestructible ultramicroscopic billiard-balls controlled by fixed unalterable laws, it may be well to recall that modern physics views the world as a spatiotemporal manifold of centres of energy and spontaneity; in such a world Jesus's resurrection may well be seen, not as a violation or an overriding of the inherent and proper workings of nature, but rather as their joyful and blessed fulfilment, in bringing nature to a perfection that it could not attain by its own efforts. More specifically, we can see the transformation and glorification of the human nature of Jesus in his resurrection as the supreme honour and privilege conferred by God on human nature as such and on the human race.

For the human body of Jesus is the place at which the eternal Son of God has, so to speak, keyed himself into the human race and so into the material universe. The resurrection and transformation of the human nature of Jesus in its totality, which the accounts in the Gospels describe, are the initiation of the transformation of the whole created world in him, the setting loose of the re-creative energy which was encapsulated in the human race when the Word became flesh in the womb of Mary. I shall not discuss here the paradox that, while in one sense everything has been done by Jesus in his resurrection, there is another sense in which everything still remains to be done in the world through his body the Church. As Vatican II was at pains to emphasise, the Church on earth is on pilgrimage, not yet in the fatherland; *in hac lacrimarum valle* we pray to him *qui vitam sine termino nobis donet in patria*. Nevertheless, God has raised

Christ from the dead and made him sit at his right hand in the heavenly places; he has raised us up with him and made us to sit with him in the heavenly places in Christ Jesus.[21] In their very different ways the two books which I have made the subject of this article should increase our understanding and our confidence in this faith.

Eric Mascall O.G.S. is an honorary assistant priest at St Mary's. He is an Emeritus Student of Christ Church, Oxford, Emeritus Professor of King's College, London, and Canon Emeritus of Truro Cathedral.

Words and the Word

W. H. Auden

IF, AS THE BIBLE TEACHES, Man is a special creature in that he is made in the image of God, then every specifically human activity must be a reflection, however distorted by sin, of some aspect of the Divine activity.

To say that Man is a special creature does not, of course, mean that he has nothing in common with the rest of creation. Composed of matter, we are subject, like all matter, to the laws of physics and chemistry; as living organisms subject, like all life, to the temporal cycle of birth, growth, reproduction, death. Thus, Genesis gives two accounts of man's creation by God. In Chapter One, 'Male and female created he them,' and said 'Be fruitful and multiply.' In Chapter Two, 'God breathed into Adam the breath of Life and he became a living soul.' And Eve is created because it is not good for man to be alone. The relation between them, that is to say, is a double one: a relation between two *individuals* of the same species determined by the reproductive instinct, and a relation between two *persons,* the nature of which depends upon their own free choices.

The term 'individual' is primarily a biological classification. A horse, a tree, a man, a woman. Secondarily, because man is a social animal and one without built-in instinctive modes of behaviour, a social-political classification: an Englishman, a Frenchman, a member of the Smith family, a doctor, a don. As individuals we are created by sexual reproduction and social conditioning. We are members of various societies not by our choice but by the accident of birth and economic necessity. We do not act; we exhibit characteristic social behaviour. We are countable, classifiable, comparable, replaceable.

As persons, each of us is created in the image of God, able to say 'I' in response to God's 'Thou' and the thous of other persons. The myth of our common descent from a single ancestor, Adam, is a way of expressing the fact that, as persons, we are called into being, not by any biological process, but by other persons, God, our parents, our siblings, our friends: each of us, in fact, is Adam, an incarnation of all mankind, the like of whom has never existed before and never will again. As persons we are not willy-nilly members of societies, but we are free to form communities, groups united, as St Augustine said, by a common love of something other than ourselves, be it God, music, stamp-collecting or what-have-you. As persons, we are capable of deeds, of choosing to do this rather than that and holding ourselves responsible for the consequences whatever they may be. As persons we are uncountable, unclassifiable, incomparable, irreplaceable.

The particular kind of personal activity I want to consider with you, because I am professionally concerned with it, is speech. Both the Old and the New Testament use the analogy of human speech in their descriptions of God as creator. 'God *said,* "Let there be light" and there was light.' 'In the beginning was the *Word,* and the Word was with God, and the Word was God. All things were made by him and without him was not anything made that was made.'

In understanding these statements, we must be careful not to confuse two ways in which we employ what we call words; our use of them as a tool, a code of communication between individuals, and our use of them as living speech between persons.

Many animals have some form of code by which members of the same species can convey to each other vital information about food, sex, territory, the presence of enemies, etc., and in social animals like the bee, this code may be extremely complex, but it remains a code, it never develops into speech. Only persons need and can develop speech for only persons can say 'I' and 'Thou' and desire freely to disclose themselves to one another and gratuitously to share in each other's experiences. To understand the true nature of human speech we must begin, not with impersonal code messages like 'The cat is on the mat' but with words of summons and response – 'Adam, where art thou?' 'Lord, here am I.', with words of command and obedience – 'Follow me.' 'Be it unto me according to thy word,' with the first and second personal pronouns, with proper names.

The first and second personal pronouns have no gender. The third has gender and for that reason should, properly speaking, be called impersonal. It is grammatically convenient when talking about someone who is not present to use the third person, and in some cultures it is polite to use it when addressing people with whom one is not on intimate terms, but to *think* of others as 'him' or 'her' instead of by their names is to think of them not as persons but as individual objects. Proper names, you may have noticed, are untranslatable. When translating into English a German novel, the hero of which is named Heinrich, the translator will retain the name; he will not turn it into Henry.

Creation by the Word of God. The analogy implies a belief that creation is an act of power or authority, not of force or violence, one in which therefore the role of the created is as essential as that of the creator. If somebody knocks me down with his fist, that is an act of violence in which I play no role. But if someone says to me 'Lie down on the ground', and I obey, the act of lying down is my act in response to his command, the authority of which I recognise.

Our relation to the Word of God is a dialogue between creature and creator, child and Father. Again, on God's side, not an exercise of force. As St Augustine said, 'He who made us without our help will not save us without our consent.' As Christ said of his parables, so says the divine Word of itself: he that hath ears to hear, let him hear.

Our relation to each other in human speech is a dialogue between neighbours. My senses tell me that the world is inhabited by a number of human individuals whom I can count and compare with each other, and I do not doubt my senses. It requires an act of faith on my part, however, to believe that each of them is, like myself, a unique person, for this my senses cannot show me. Conversely, my own personal existence is to me self-evident; what in my case calls for faith is to believe when confronted by my reflection in the mirror that the features I see are really mine, that I, too, am an individual member of the human race like other folks.

The sin of pride is essentially the refusal to make this double act of faith, to regard my neighbour as an object, an object of interest or desire maybe, but still an object, and to regard myself as an autonomous God. It is not in my power to decide what emotions shall be aroused in me by others, though by proper direction of my attention, my emotions may change. I cannot be commanded to like X or to fall in love with Y. Nor can I be commanded to deny my personal existence. What is in my power to do or refuse to do and can therefore be the subject of a command, is to love my neighbour as myself, for my love of myself is not, strictly speaking, an emotion at all, but a recognition that I exist.

To the degree that we fail, and to some degree we all fail, to love our neighbours as ourselves, no genuine speech is possible between us. Where love of God and neighbour are lacking, speech very soon degenerates into self-propaganda and violent verbal noises. Propaganda does not seek for a response; it demands a tautological echo. Pride neither speaks nor listens; it unceasingly advertises itself. If I regard my neighbour as an object to manipulate then the truth or the exact meaning of what I say to him is irrelevant, and very soon I shall lack the power of speaking either truthfully or precisely. One has only to glance at a newspaper to see the consequences.

The Christian Church came into being at Pentecost. The gift of the Holy Spirit on that occasion is generally called the gift of tongues, but it might equally well be called the gift of ears. One might say that, for the first time, Parthians and Medes, Elamites and the dwellers in Mesopotamia and in Judea and Cappadocia, strangers from Rome, Jews and proselytes, Cretes and Arabians, were able to listen when a foreigner was speaking. The curse of Babel is not the fact that there are many languages – diversity is always a good – but the attitude implied by defining a barbarian as someone who does not speak Greek. As Sir William Osler said: half of us are blind, few of us feel, and we are all deaf. As writers, readers, human beings, we cannot speak to or understand each other unless we are first prepared to listen. Of all the gifts which the Holy Spirit is able to bestow, the one for which we should first and most earnestly pray is humility of ear.

W. H. Auden had been an undergraduate at Christ Church. As Professor of Poetry at Oxford he often stayed there and, in his last years, he was invited to live in a house in the College.

The soul of man

Ulrich Simon

IN 1932 ALDOUS HUXLEY published his *Brave New World*. One of the slogans by which the management voice their contempt for the past reads like this; 'There was a thing called the soul and a thing called immortality.' The implication is: there was, but there no longer is, a thing called the soul. In his Foreword of 1946[1] Huxley comments on the fulfilment of his feared utopian prophecies. *Si monumentum requiris circumspice.* The gutted cities of Europe and Japan witness to the triumph of science and social control mechanism. Huxley warns against the militarised supernational totalitarianism with a motto taken from Nicholas Berdiaeff, *'La vie marche vers les utopies'* and he looks forward to *'un siècle où les intellectuels et la classe cultivée rêveront aux moyens d'éviter les utopies.'* A less perfect society is needed to secure a free society. But a free society presupposes the autonomy of the human soul.

This issue was brought home to me forcibly a few years ago when I chanced to read Bruno Bettelheim's monograph on the English translations of Sigmund Freud's works.[2] He demonstates there, at some length and in great detail, that the Anglo-American translators have deliberately distorted the text and thereby forged psychology and psychoanalysis into a weapon against the existence of the soul. Bettelheim argues, I think convincingly, that Freud, though hardly a protagonist of religion or idealism, meant his work to be therapeutic for the soul. If you like, Freud started a process of curing souls. More important, his psychosomatic findings and treatments did not proceed as if man had no such thing as the soul. The impact of rendering *Seele* not with soul, but with Mind, has been far-reaching. The reader not only of translations of Freud but also of post-Freudian psychology and the student of medical psychiatry take it for granted that the unconscious-subconscious resides in the physical.

This murder of the soul naturally derives from those whom it serves most, namely the dictators and the butchers of humanity, for where the soul does not exist you can kill without pangs of conscience or a fear of what may come after death. Dante knew that the state of hell is bereft of penitence, and in our century the torturers of mankind no longer acknowledge that man is sacred because he is a living soul. Michael Scammell's *Solzhenitsyn,*[3] especially the procedure of arrest and investigation in the Lubyanka, shows how the prisoner has become a thing.

Western technocrats, too, despatch the soul in their worlds of computers and cloned species. None of this need cause us surprise. However, the extinction of the soul from Christian discourse and from the Church's awareness must make us pause. It has come about for allegedly scholarly insights. The Hebrew terms, it has been said, should be freed from Greek overtones. This leads, as with Freud, to new linguistic conventions. Take *nephesh chaiah*, the living soul, which God creates by blowing the breath of life into the matter, into dust. In and through this dynamic act of creation man comes to reflect the divine form. Accordingly to the Greek translators the corresponding meaning is expressed by '*Kai egeneto ho anthropos eis psychen zosan*'. So also the Vulgate perpetuated what was to become the dogmatic stance of orthodox belief: '*Et factus est homo in animam viventem.*' Here we have the *anima* which was assumed also by pagans to be free and immortal; for example, the famous address which Hadrian is supposed to have composed in AD 138 to his dying soul (and which Byron translated freely):

Animula vagula blandula	Ah! gentle, fleeting, wav'ring sprite,
Hospes comesque corporis,	Friend and associate of this clay!
Quae nunc abibis in loca	To what unknown region borne,
Pallidula rigida nudula,	Wilt thou now wing thy distant flight?
Nec ut soles dabis iocos!	No more with wonted humour gay,
	But pallid, cheerless, and forlorn.

It is not too much to claim that the Christian message was to transform the expectation of the soul freed from the body after death. Through and with Christ all could be bliss and joy everlasting, a participation of glory. Thus ordinary mortals greet their reunion after death. Graffiti in the catacombs express this hope not only for the martyrs but for all the baptised.

Yet modern translators want to get away from such a positive and individualistic eschatology. They allege that 'soul' runs against Hebraic this-worldly corporateness. At least that is the argument, and the fruits thereof can now be studied in such translations as the New English Bible, the Jerusalem Bible, the Good News Bible and many other versions. There is no absolute consistency. Take again Genesis 2.7, which in JB ends with 'thus man became a living being'. In the NEB the translators agree on 'the man became a living creature'. We can see the problem, of course. If 'living soul' is really now meaningless or conjures up a kind of ghost or shadowy vapour another word must be found. Martin Buber seems to have felt this here, rendering *'der Mensch wurde zum lebenden Wesen'*, which retains a mysterious and ontological ring, more definite and precise than the rather vague 'being'. Psalm 22.21, *'Rette meine* Seele *vorm Schwert'* shows Buber's sensitive response to the translator's task.

The problem, then, is not one of Hebraic versus Greek psychology or understanding of man. There is not the slightest evidence that the Hebrew writers and traditionalists eschewed a belief in the soul, and the modern translators should not be allowed to hide behind a quasi-scientific screen of ethnic culture. The Jewish liturgy could not include the following prayer at the Morning Service unless the worshippers believed in the autonomy of the soul.

O my God, the soul which thou gavest me is pure;
thou didst create it, thou didst form it,
thou didst breathe it into me. Thou preservest
it within me, and thou wilt take it from me,
but wilt restore it unto me hereafter.
So long as the soul is within me, I will give thanks
unto thee, O Lord my God and God of my Fathers.
Sovereign of all works, Lord of all souls!
Blessed art thou, O Lord, who restoreth souls unto the dead.

This is not the place to make a thorough examination of all the instances in which *'nephesh'* and *'psyche'* challenge the translator's art and his exegetical purpose. A few examples will suffice. In Genesis 42.21 Joseph's brothers no longer regard Joseph's 'anguish of soul' but recall 'whose suffering we saw' in the NEB. In Numbers 15.28 atonement is not made for the soul but for the 'said individual' or just 'the person' in JB. The NEB changes 'bitterness of soul' to 'deep distress' in 1 Samuel 1.10 and in 1 Kings 17.21 the child's 'soul' does not return but its 'breath of life'. The rejection of the lyrical note becomes very pronounced in the Psalms: God does not restore 'my soul' (23.3) nor lift up 'my soul' (25.1), nor does 'my soul wait' (62.5) nor is 'my soul brought out of prison' but subject or object are 'me', 'my heart', and in Ezekiel 3.19 just 'self'. The same tendency can be studied in New Testament phrases, where 'soul' again is replaced by 'heart', 'life', 'self'. In Luke 2.35 a sword will not pierce 'through thy own soul also', but merely 'you too'. Such a prosaic bathos proves, I think, that we are concerned with more than painstaking and pedantic comparisons.

Inconsistency marks the translators' preferences. In the important passage about priorities – 'What shall it profit a man if he shall gain the whole world and lose his own soul?' (Mark 8,36-7) the NEB gives us 'true self' and the JB and GNB simply 'life'. But 'life' in this context is wildly misleading, for it is precisely the 'soul' as the bearer and meaning of life in the face of oppression which has to be heroically defended. In I Peter 2.11 this seems to be accepted when all the translations are content to underline the struggle between the lust of the flesh and the soul's integrity. More important, during the Agony in Gethsemane, Jesus is still seen to be exceedingly sorrowful in his soul. Nor is it denied to the martyrs that, although they cannot prevent their bodies from being killed, their *psyche* remains inviolate. Perhaps one cannot aim at complete consistency in the sense of a philosophical definition when in a document like Hebrews the writer refers to the division of *psyche* and *pneuma,* the dividing asunder of soul and spirit (Hebrews 4.12), which NEB rejects in favour of 'life and spirit'.

The problem is not a new one. How do we relate 'body' and

'soul'? Most people accept the coinherence and the separateness of body and soul. When the BCP formulates 'The body of our Lord Jesus Christ which was given for thee preserve thy body and soul' the recipient hardly reflects on the dualistic nature of himself. Yet, it is hinted at and perhaps even offers a way into the complexity of Christology, the two natures of Christ.

Some Christian schools of thought have been perfectly happy with a dualistic understanding of man. Without going so far as to regard the body merely as a tomb or a tent which the soul enters and then leaves they went along with the Platonic claim that the soul is autonomous and responsible and hence immortal. The arguments proferred in the *Phaedo* and the *Phaedrus* were accepted by Philo even before the Christian fathers and teachers adapted them to their systems. I wonder how they would react to a careful estimate by John L. McKenzie, SJ in his *Dictionary of the Bible*[4] who concludes in his article on *Soul* that Platonic concepts must be jettisoned in favour of 'psycho-physical totality', describing 'the concrete manner and condition of being'. Thus he arrives at 'self or person', distinct from other selves, the conscious subject of action and passion. 'Perhaps the ego of modern psychology. . .' comes nearest our need, but this modernism makes McKenzie curiously extreme in the interpretation of New Testament usage of *Psyche*. The salvation of the soul becomes a supernatural and discontinuous event. Distinguished biblical scholars do not always make good philosophers and fall into unsuspected traps. 'Conscious subject of action and passion', it must be emphasised, must exclude a lot of people, especially babies and young children.

The intellectual traps are manifold. First of all, there is the charge that the soul is a primitive projection of some sort, perhaps brought to the West from Shamans, that it has something to do with breathing, and therefore also breathing one's last. Hence the soul belongs to that nebulous assortment of goods which men wish to have in order to survive. Thus John Hick in *Death and Eternal Life*[5] discusses 'soul' as a 'value word' and finds it wanting in connection with 'the random character of the process of meiosis in the formation of the individual sperm cell . . . . selected to fertilise an ovum? He therefore gently concedes that to 'speak of man as a soul is to speak mythologically'. 'Soul is a valuing name for the self.' But we are not spared the whole chain of being from foetus to babyhood to personhood, man in the making; a soul or *'atman'* refers to the ideal state of human consciousness. But curiously this is realised by negating individual egoity. Hick does not like Rahner's hypothesis of the pancosmic state of the soul after death, but at least he takes seriously the rejected doctrines of the pre-existence and the transmigration of souls. His global view compels Hick to remain open to, and yet unconvinced of, the soul's immortality.

One cannot help being amazed at Aldous Huxley's prophetic anticipation of our mental and material state. He saw that the totalitarian 'happiness' would be buttressed by genetic engineering. His cloned Alphas, Betas, Gammas, Deltas are made by men, so how should they have divine souls? Now this fiction has been translated into scientific fact. Hence even the traditional theologian bows to DNA. Thus Paul Badham in the recent *Dictionary of Christian Theology*[6] refers to 'advances in evolutionary biology, genetics and neurophysiology along with the philosophical analysis of the concept of a person' which has led many to question the validity of soul language. Yet courageously Badham also says that 'belief in the soul would appear to remain essential'.

Clearly our point of view is either determined by the experience of test-tube babies and the dialectical materialism of Marxist-Leninist socialism, or by a totally different experience of man as the intended image of God in the face of Jesus Christ. It is absurd to relegate the soul as a kind of ballast taken over from Plato. How can it be that not only Christians, but also Jews and Moslems acknowledge the individual soul to be the king and ruler of the body, the principle of life, the power of organisation and perception, the rider of the steed, the captain of the ship, the governor of a state, but a stranger on earth, yearning for the supernal home, immortal in its search for moral and intellectual perfection?

This must not be taken as a rhetorical question. If the soul is in some way created by and for God such a truth is universal. But its universality is cut short and thrown out by genetics and totalitarian rule. We are not concerned with a defence of Platonism in Christianity; rather, Plato in the *Timaeus,* the *Republic,* the *Phaedo* and the *Phaedrus* underpins the universal belief that there is an *atem* or *anima* in us which shares and corresponds to the universal breath of life. We affirm certain analogies which, we feel, point towards the autonomy of the soul and yet also dwell upon its vulnerability and contingent existence. Thus, with Goethe, we take comfort from the phenomenon of the butterfly, a symbol of change and growth towards splendour from humble beginnings and apparent sleep. Again the spark of fire becomes an image of the individual passion and warmth which have their centre in something greater than themselves. Thus we approach the traditional pattern, both of reflection and correspondence, in which purification and illumination lead to the apex of perfect spiritualisation. This is the ascent of the soul which not only theologians but poets celebrate as the meaning of life, when, for example, they cite the glory of the lark ascending.

Perhaps the most impressive simile for the soul is water. *'Des Menschen Seele gleicht dem Wasser . . . '* begins Goethe's Song of the Spirits over the Waters. Man's soul is like water: from heaven it comes, to heaven it rises, and to earth again it must descend, moving to and fro for ever. For Goethe the soul is decidedly not a static entity, but a dynamic force which actively and passively moves and changes. The key is to be found in eternal transformation, for, as Goethe claims, without the dying and becoming man is but a sad guest on earth. Goethe supplies therefore an important dialectical foil to the conception of the soul as something merely given and then given up at death. Plato's autonomy of the soul needs to be balanced by this painful but necessary fact which none other than St Paul continually emphasises, namely, that the soul is not yet made perfect.

In what other way can we describe the moral, intellectual, and aesthetic vocation of the soul, the heart of man's response to God and his economy? After all, the body of man is also continually changing, again like water, but this metabolism on the physical plane cannot aspire to perfection. On the contrary,

The soul of man

it heads towards its decline, to decay and death. The body has no moral, intellectual, and aesthetic vocation as such, except, of course, to serve and enable the soul to ascend to the ideal.

How does the soul attain to goodness, truth and beauty? Here we enter the mysterious realm of grace, which even non-Christians are aware of, though their answers differ from the Christian tradition. According to the latter the grace bestowed at baptism and sustained by the Holy Spirit enables the soul to pray for illumination and thence for the desire to know and thence to practise the good. For the Christian the knowledge and practice is inseparable from the imitation of Christ and a sacramental coinherence. The secularist jumps the religious hurdle and, following Kant in particular, acknowledges the force of the conscience within and the witness of the cosmic order outside – the heavens above. But religious or secular, the soul is affected by the direction of the will and is trained, while training itself, in the discipline of a transcendent moral duty: not my will, but your will be done!

Whereas Kant maintained the objectivity of the categorical imperative and accordingly of the will his contemporaries favoured a subjective definition of beauty and truth. Hume authenticated a subjective empiricism, 'Beauty in things exists in the mind which contemplates them', from which Keats' famous lines 'Beauty is truth, truth beauty' may derive the notion that this is all we know on earth and all we need to know. It is a dangerous doctrine for it lays burdens on the soul which cannot be borne.

Poets, however, do not aim at consistency, and Keats, so young and doomed to die so soon, cannot be accused of abusing the soul's ideal search for truth and for beauty as abiding ideals. 'Half in love with easeful death' he listens to the nightingale, the soul pouring forth abroad in such ecstasy. Once you admit the inward strain you are overpowered by the soul's multiple activity and passivity. It is the soul which voices plaints and joys, is abused by self, redeemed by generosity, seduced by error, ambushed by light, lost and won. The progress of the deathless soul (Donne) is certainly chequered, it is an 'enchanted boat' (Shelley). Even the atheist cherishes his soul as separate from himself, an entity to be addressed, pitied, mourned, and encouraged.

The worst thing that can befall mankind is the dedication of souls to nothing, for nothing in this respect means evil, falsehood, and ugliness. 'The true strength of guilty kings,' warns Matthew Arnold, is to be felt 'when they corrupt the souls of those they rule.' Lucky Arnold who did not live in our century when this corruption is systematic and institutionalised. Its apex is reached when the existence of the soul is squeezed out of human reality. The Christian Church is now placed in an Elijah-like position: either Baal or God, either the corporate State, entertainment, sport, propaganda or the Soul, created by and destined for God.

The treachery of Christians to their own souls becomes evident when they subscribe to all the modern horrors of compulsion. Translations of texts may seem to be trivial in the context of the brutalism of our times. But they are indicative of something much deeper. In the Christian context you delete the soul's identity, the face radiating the eternal Spirit, and you are left without identity, with absence and impersonal institutions. Ironically the representatives of the soulless Christianity are the very people who mouth the word love and endlessly bully us to pay them and their social causes. Now love, whatever definition or aspect of *agape* you immediately respond to, is unthinkable in terms of groups, classes, and races, or, indeed, institutions. The mysterious bond which unites man and woman, parents and children, friends, and even enemies is nourished and sustained by the abiding reality which is the soul. The address 'Thou' and 'Thee', expressed in baptism, confirmation, communion, penance is not directed to nameless groups but to the named soul, at the beginning and at the end of this earthly life. Will the sheep going astray now at last return to the shepherd and bishop of their souls?

The pious fraud of collectivism and the jargon of sociological Christianity must be attacked by the 'dialectic of the heart', namely, the soul's movement towards God from the world. The soul has to learn to appropriate forms of this speech, for it can only advance in the 'vale of soul making' (Keats) by receiving nourishment from the Spirit of God. This happens in a thousand different ways, but, above all, the education of the soul requires silence. The shattering noise of our world is soulless and kills our humanity. The soul belongs to and thrives in the absolute silence of God. The harmony of immortal souls, as Lorenzo tells Jessica in *The Merchant of Venice,* is cosmic and all-pervading, but 'we cannot hear it'. But given silence we do hear it, see it, and love it. Then, as the old slogan has it, we can exclaim, 'Why, bless my soul . . .'

For Christians this education of the soul begins and ends with prayer. In many tongues the soul asserts its autonomy. In spiritual anguish the cry goes up from the deep: *'Jesu, der Du meine Seele . . .'*, recalling the whole past of redemption. The relative clause should be noted by the butchers of liturgical language who have destroyed the cosmic coherence of the spiritual universe. The prayers for the departed touch the heart of the matter. 'We offer to thee, O Lord, sacrifices and prayers: do thou receive them in behalf of those souls whom we commemorate . . . Grant them to pass from death to life.' Or, as generations have prayed, *'Fac eas, Domine, de morte transire ad vitam!'*

Ulrich Simon is Professor Emeritus, London University and former Dean of King's College, London.

The four last things

Martin Israel

THE LAST THINGS in any individual life are death and judgement followed by hell or heaven as the case may be. It is a consideration of these that brings us close to the mystery of the second coming of Christ.

★　★　★

Death in one respect is the moment of dramatic closure of our life on earth, but on a deeper level it is a state of continual preparation for the great moment of truth ahead of us each moment of our mortal life. Indeed, the very moment that heralds our life is also preparing us for death. Death seen in this light becomes not so much a severing event as a distillation of the whole process of our earthly life, our incarnation, for that moment of separation from the physical body, when it may be surveyed in the cold scrutiny of eternity. If we can see our period of incarnation as a preparation for the great work ahead of us in the eternal spheres, we will come to acknowledge death as the time of transition from the temporal to the eternal, from the spatial to the infinite. All this, of course, requires faith, and it is here that the great religions of the world have their wisdom to impart, a wisdom, however, that can only be truly assimilated by those who are in close contact with the source of their own being, which is usefully called the soul.

We are, in fact, building up the body that will accompany us in the life beyond death even now, in our mortal life, according to our attitudes and actions. This spiritual body that envelops the seat of our true being, the soul, is composed of our thoughts and our relations with other people. We are enjoined in our Faith especially to remember God at the time of our death, but this is unlikely to be a strong prerogative if we are not with God continually in our thoughts and actions during our active life here and now, a life that may be terminated at any time by the inroads of a sudden accident or illness. No one knows when his last moment of mortal life is to be, therefore he who is wise is with God perpetually in his thoughts, even when his actions may necessarily be very mundane indeed. We are, in fact, with God whenever we behave with justice and compassion towards our fellow creatures in the present moment. Indeed, de Caussade's 'sacrament of the present moment' guides the lives of all aware, thoughtful people, who remember that they lie in the divine dispensation every moment of their lives. This does not imply that God is a sort of Big Brother in terms of George Orwell's *1984*, a monster who watches us continually and punishes any contravention of his immutable law with ferocious cruelty. It tells us rather that in God is the atmosphere of freedom, love and growth into the persons we are destined to become provided we enter into his providence with trust and humility. The actual moment of transition may well be less cataclysmic than we are wont to imagine, and what we are in essence, we may well find ourselves immersed in on the other side of death. If we can bring the divine thought with us, we will find ourselves encompassed in the divine love, but that divine thought may not be so easy to conjure up at the time of our demise if our previous style of life has been essentially selfish and predatory. This, in fact, I believe is the nature of the judgement ahead of us.

If my life has been one long saga of selfishness in which my personal relationships have been used entirely to my mundane benefit with no account of the well-being of the other people involved, if indeed I have used other people voraciously for my own selfish ends and then discarded them on the scrap-heap of forgotten things in my onward thrust for power, when the time for my departure comes, I will have to part with whatever worldly gain I had achieved and enter into a realm of values rather than things. It is indeed a terrible reflection on the low level of human awareness that this life is linked to possessions and power rather than the soul and its growth into spiritual maturity. When we die we can in truth take nothing with us other than what we have achieved on a spiritual level; the earthly remains of our incarnation are left to those who succeed us, and soon we are forgotten on this level. We are judged quite spontaneously and inevitably by what we have sown in terms of living relationships, primarily with our fellow humans but also with the other forms of life on our small but very important planet. If we have lived well on a spiritual level, there will be many who will be available to greet us when we make the great transition of death. Thus a person of little account in the world's estimation of power and general significance but one who has lived in peace and inner integrity with his neighbours, will be greeted with acclaim on the other side of death, for he will be clad in a radiant spiritual body composed of all his past deeds and attitudes. On the other hand, a person who has shone in the world's estimation on account of the show he has made in some specialised field while his private life has been a saga of cruelty to those around him, will find himself with a poor spiritual body and no one to greet him in death's country. St John of the Cross says that when the evening comes we will be judged on love. Then indeed all our scintillating worldly possessions will lie in the dust of memory, and all that remains is the soul, which has either been enriched through life's many encounters or else lies as undeveloped as it was during the period of our infancy. In this respect we remember Jesus's teaching that we have to receive the Kingdom of God as a little child, but here he is speaking of innocence and a sense of perpetual wonder that is part of a child's consciousness. In our life this beautiful soul quality of the little child has to be balanced by the service and self-sacrifice that is part of the adult period of our life. To the child the whole world revolves around his wishes and demands; only later does he learn to respect other individuals' right to exist also. If we, despite the calls of life and its stringent demands, can retain something of the childlike innocence that was ours many years previously, then indeed we are in the Kingdom of God even in this world.

I am convinced that when we die our inner consciousness will be very like what we were before death, except that there will no longer be any encompassing physical body behind with which to conceal our inner attitudes. In the Collect for Purity that introduces the Anglican Eucharist we pray to 'Almighty God, to whom all hearts are open, all desires known, and from whom no secrets are hidden.' In the afterlife this situation is one we have to confront just as those around us see it also. Therefore it is good if we can come to terms with the fullness of our psychic life, unconscious as well as conscious, while we are still alive in the flesh. In such a situation of inner enlightenment there will be less trauma when we have died and also less remedial work to be done on the other side of death.

★　★　★

Judgement will be related to the reception we enjoy on the other side of death together with a realisation of the quality of the spiritual body that encompasses the naked soul-mind complex, for now the physical body has gone back to the earth from which it was fashioned in the first case.

Will we know Christ directly when we enter this communal type of judgement? I believe that we will indeed encounter our Lord then, but he will not show himself as a person, as the Jesus of Nazareth whom his contemporaries knew so well two thousand years ago. Already after the resurrection his appearance had changed so that he was no longer directly recognisable to Mary of Magdala, the disciples or those on the road to Emmaus: there had to be some special gesture or word for them to recognise the risen Lord. After the ascension he is seated in unity with the Father, and now he comes to us as radiant light of uncreated nature; the Damascus Road appearance to St Paul is typical. We will know him in the life beyond death as an atmosphere of radiance and warmth that will speak to our innermost self, reminding us of the words of the Fourth Gospel that God is a spirit and those that worship him must worship him in spirit and in truth. In his presence we will know the categorical verdict of our lives on earth and be prepared for the way ahead. In the divine nature mercy is always tempered with justice, but the justice is not an arbitrary verdict of God, whose nature is pure love. It is the justice that is inherent in the created order, known universally as the law of cause and effect. As St Paul puts it, 'We should not be deceived, God is not mocked, for as a man sows, so shall he reap.' Fortunately, forgiveness is essential to the divine nature, but we have to be open to receive that forgiveness, and this means an acknowledgement of our past sinfulness and an earnest commitment to an amended life. Unawareness and pride are the two important stumbling blocks to our receiving the full grace of God.

★   ★   ★

Hell is a state of complete isolation from the company, indeed the fellowship, of our fellow creatures and from the presence of God. At the same time one is horrifyingly aware of one's own isolation; in other words, the awareness of one's own identity remains, but it is absolutely isolated. A reasonable earthly analogy would be imprisonment in caves without illumination where one's cries for help simply return to one as echoes without reference to anybody outside being so much as aware of one's plight. Another analogy would be incarceration in a lift between floors after everyone else had left for the evening. One would have to wait until the next day for relief, and a terrible claustrophobia would soon overcome one. In hell it is our own past life and present attitude that isolate us from God and our fellows; until we have repented and confessed our sinful ways there can be no help available. There is much in the gospel narrative to suggest that the state of hell is irreversible, that the gulf between the saved and unsaved is unbridgeable, but such a view negates the love of God. In the Eucharist we affirm that his nature is always to have mercy, a quality brought out especially well in the three parables of Luke 15 (which culminates in the parable of the Prodigal Son). We cannot plumb the depth of this mystery except by groping into the depths of our own hearts, when we realise that we too, even if we are sincere believers, have been at times great sinners. Who indeed can ultimately be saved? I am myself persuaded that the soul is immortal because God has created it, and he loves all created things. While I have no doubt that we can be in hell interminably according to our own disposition whether in this life or the life beyond death, I cannot believe that the God of love can consign any of his creatures eternally to hell without reference to any repentance on their part. This view of salvation depends as much on the disposition of the creature as the magnanimity of the Creator. And here we have to leave the debate.

Once the creature has seen the magnitude of his sinfulness I believe he is tractable to the love of God, brought down to him conceivably in the form of members of the Communion of Saints and the angelic hierarchy, and now can start the upward journey to a knowledge of God. This is the intermediate state traditionally called purgatory in Catholic theology. It is the plane of purgation, in which all deleterious past attitudes are brought fully to consciousness and their fruits bitterly repented of. We have to live out many past episodes that we would rather have permanently forgotten, but we have to come to terms with the eternal law of life, which is confession for past sins and a growth into a new awareness of the unity that brings all disparate elements of life close to God, the universal creator. Is the believer exempted from all this suffering? I believe not, but the presence of the spirit of Christ guides and sustains him through all the travail. The analogy here would be a Christian who has committed a frightful crime. Confession and the sacrament of penance would not clear him of his guilt, which would have to be confessed to the appropriate legal authorities. Even if the judge were a believer also, he would be compelled to administer the appropriate punishment, which might well include a long term of imprisonment. But the period of incarceration would be one of blessing inasmuch as Christ would be with the prisoner, who would emit a spiritual radiance that could help many of his fellow prisoners in the darkness of their cells. With the Spirit of the Lord close to one any punishment takes on something of the nature of a blessing, and one learns the important spiritual truth that we are all parts of the one body, which is God's creation over which he in his threefold nature takes undisputed charge. The same argument applies to a believer in this life who is incurably ill with a progressive, painful disease which remains intractable even to spiritual forms of healing. When Christ is with him in spirit, his own spirit is raised up to heaven, and he can be the instrument of bringing many others, including unbelievers, to a new realisation of reality. All this is part of the healing and transfiguration of the soul both in this life and the life beyond death.

Jesus speaks of there being many mansions, or resting-places, in his Father's Kingdom. William Temple in his *Readings from St John's Gospel*, compares these to wayside caravanserais – shelters or stages along the road where travellers may rest on their journey. It is probable that the soul, progressively cleared of much superficial dross, moves from one psychical state to another in which it gradually comes more to what it was meant to be. What these stages may be and in what medium they may occur is outside our span of knowledge, and indeed too much speculation about these matters may be deleterious inasmuch as it tends to concentrate our attention on matters far outside our immediate action, so that we get seduced into vain imaginings instead of applying ourselves to the matters in hand, namely integrity in our present labours and proper relationships with those in our vicinity.

★ ★ ★

Heaven is a state of complete openness to our fellows and to the love of God. It is the direct antithesis to hell, where one is enclosed and isolated. In heaven we cease to guard our individual identity, for we are in truth all parts of the one body whose name is Christ. We now have nothing to hide, while at the same time can include all facets of the people around us in absolute love. Heaven, like hell, is a state of being that we can experience in this life here and now no less than in the life beyond death. It does not depend on the perfection of our character so much as our immediate openness to God's presence, whose nature is love. God does not love us because we are worthy but because he made us. Thus in the parable of the Publican and the Pharisee the sinful publican is in better relationship with God than the self-righteous Pharisee, despite the fact that the Pharisee is much more worthy in terms of the world's judgement than the publican, who has nothing to recommend him apart from the sudden shaft of insight into his own extreme unworthiness which made him submit himself unconditionally to God. In that act of submission he was rendered open to his fellow creatures also, whereas the Pharisee's very excellence by worldly standards separated him both from God and from his fellow creatures. The experience of heaven often follows unconditional forgiveness; then we cease to think about ourselves at all, and can flow out in love to all around us.

Such an experience of heaven is inevitably transitory. We have to descend to earth once more, and then the heavenly glow of eternity is lost. Only the saint can retain something of that glow during the course of this mortal life, and even then it may be scarcely possible in a Gethsemane type of situation. Indeed, it is doubtful whether any person can know heaven with any degree of constancy until he has traversed his garden of Gethsemane. Then at last he is no longer anchored to self and can flow out without reserve to all his fellow men, indeed to all that lives. I have no doubt that the great saints are in a condition of heaven perpetually, and in prayer they can come to our assistance. It is fallacious, I am convinced, to see heaven as a static realm inhabited by the blessed where they enjoy the uninterrupted presence of Christ and have passed beyond any concern for the vast concourse of creatures outside the pale. On the other hand, it is much more probable that they are continually about their Father's business in bringing help and understanding to all those in the intermediate levels as well as to us on earth, whose spiritual condition, in any case, mirrors that of the vast company in the life beyond death. My conviction about the essential mobility and concern of the blessed ones is that no one can be in a state of unconditional bliss when even one of the number of created persons is in hell. That we are all parts of the one body, a doctrine enunciated so cogently by St Paul in his letter to the Ephesians and repeated in one way or another by the mystics of all the great world religions, brings with it the realisation of our absolute interdependence. Therefore there can be no permanent, let alone perpetual heaven, while even one of us is in pain. The compassion evinced by the saints is not only a part of their intrinsic spirituality, it is also evidence that their great work is to bring all rational creatures to the knowledge and love of God with whom they are in such intimate communion.

It has to be faced, however, that not all creatures are prepared to leave their abode in hell. Pride, often the by-product of intense resentment, can keep one isolated, impervious to the downpour of love from on high. The tragedy of those imprisoned in hell is not the divine wrath which will not desist in its punishment but the absolute intransigence of the creature that makes it reject all overtures of love from God as relayed from the mighty Communion of Saints and doubtless the ministry of angels also. Just as we can take a horse to the water but cannot force it to drink, so we cannot compel a closed person to accept our love. This is the perpetual tragedy of hell: the enclosure of the creature refusing to acknowledge the unremitting love of God. An impasse is reached, for God's love can never be quelled, while the God-given free will allows the recalcitrant creature to reject it indefinitely. The hope is that the self-inflicted suffering of hell may eventually make the creature relent; the hope here is based on the mystical truth that each one of us contains a spark of the divine in the depth (or ground) of the soul. Eventually the 'spirit' of the soul will make its presence and authority felt and then redemption will occur. St Augustine himself acknowledged that the soul is restless until it finds its rest in God. But when will this occur on a universal as opposed to a merely personal level? And can the souls of the 'departed' be categorically separated from those of us still incarnate in this world?

★ ★ ★

The hope of a second coming of Christ is cogent here. In one respect he is always coming in glory in the awakened soul. The cosmic Christ sits in glory beyond and over the entire created universe, which includes not only the world known to the astronomer but also the intermediate psychic realm of the souls of the departed and the angelic hierarchy. He is also immanent in the human soul, fully active in those who have awakened and are doing God's work of healing in our world and no doubt the world beyond death. But until he shows himself in incontrovertible glory the universe will continue in its perverse ways. St Paul speaks rather vaguely about a final mystery when we shall not all die but instead be instantaneously lifted up to eternity. Such a prophecy is confusing when attached to a particular time, for it in fact transcends time and is of the nature of eternity. I believe that there is some aspect of time and space in the realms beyond death, even though these dimensions cannot be accurately compared with earthly time and space. But the coming of Christ in the universe is beyond time and space; it is the point of intersection of time and eternity, a mode of being that is outside the time-space universe. When it occurs, when Christ finally manifests himself in the world, matter will be transformed into spirit and death will finally be overcome by victory. Then the entire cosmos will be transformed and the physical world will be spiritualised as was the earthly body of Jesus at the time of the resurrection. Then even heaven will be transfigured in a fresh radiance. 'Heaven and earth will pass away, but my words will never pass away.' The nature of the final coming, a better expression than merely a second coming, is beyond our grasp, but I am convinced it will be of cosmic scope so that no one will be able to miss it or escape its consequences. There will be a final reconciliation of all things so that God may be all in all. Darkness and light will be finally brought into harmony, and the creation willed by God transfigured and spiritualised.

Martin Israel is a registered medical practitioner and priest-in-charge of Holy Trinity with All Saints, Prince Consort Road. He is the author of many books including Coming in Glory *(Darton, Longman and Todd, 1986).*

Where is purgatory?

Brian Horne

I COULD NOT HAVE BEEN more than ten or eleven years old when I came across a little book of private prayers that intrigued me. It belonged to one of my Roman Catholic schoolfriends and why he chose to show me his little manual of devotion I cannot now remember: like most schoolboys we were reluctant to talk about religion and, indeed, were not encouraged to do so by our parents. Perhaps we were disputing the rival claims of Rome and Canterbury and the little mass-book had been produced as part of the evidence. The liturgical reforms of the Second Vatican Council were still a long way in the future so the little mass-book was full of sentimental and lurid devotions; heady mixtures calculated to inflame the religious passions of a pious schoolboy. I thought I knew all there was to know about piety having already been confirmed at, what everybody rather disapprovingly told me, was a precociously early age; but I had never seen anything like this. Some things in it fascinated me, some repelled me (the grotesque illustrations of the Sacred Heart), and some merely puzzled me. Particularly mystifying were references to something called 'indulgences' and promises of granting indulgences if certain pious actions were properly performed. Statements like these had not appeared in any prayer book I had ever seen; perhaps I was missing out on something. I was intrigued and wanted an explanation. It was not forthcoming: the garbled answers to my questions given to me by the owner of the prayer book suggested, despite his protestations to the contrary, that he was as puzzled as I was. Definitions of the words supplied by my battered schoolboy dictionary only spread the fog of confusion, and even the Shorter Oxford English

Dictionary, which I tracked down to a dim corner of the school library, brought me no nearer enlightenment. I did not know any Roman Catholic priests at that time and I suspected that the Anglican priests I knew would either be suspicious of my questions or be as uninformed on the matter as I was. Then, as my pre-adolescent religious fervour swiftly declined, so did my interest in the curious phrases, and it was not until I was an undergraduate beginning to take an interest in medieval history that the words returned redolent with the puzzlement of childhood. 'Plenary indulgences,' said the historian, 'were offered to all those taking part in the Crusades.' Only then did I make the connection that had escaped me as a child: that the Roman Catholic doctrine of indulgences had something to do with the much broader notion of purgatory.

Purgatory is not a popular subject. I do not recall ever having heard anyone preaching about it, and I suspect that even in old-fashioned Roman Catholic pulpits it is seldom mentioned. There is an embarrassment about it, and this embarrassment is a curious state of affairs when it is examined. The Church in the West still celebrates, on the Second of November, the feast of All Souls; and at the heart of this celebration is the belief that all who have been baptised in the name of Christ, and who have not rejected him, are united, across the barriers of space and time, with one another in him who is Lord and Saviour. But there is more: such is the intimacy of our union with him and with one another in his body that we know that what is said and done by us in our lives on earth, affects those who are dead; that our requiem masses are not merely nostalgic memorial services which indulge wistful recollections of former, happier days, but are real offerings of love and prayer on behalf of those who have gone into the silence of God. If this is true, then it means that, whether we accept the elaborate paraphernalia of indulgences or not, we believe, in some way or other, in purgatory. Part of the problem is that the word has been so misused, by Catholics and Protestants alike, down the centuries, that it has become a fearsome word in Catholic mouths and a hateful word in Protestant ears. What terrors have not been conjured up in melodramatic exaggeration to frighten the feeble-minded into salvation? And what anti-Catholic hatred has not been stirred up by uninformed denunciation of this doctrine? While in reality (and this is why its loss is tragic), when properly understood, it is neither fearsome nor hateful: it is a noble and humane belief.

Two false notions about purgatory must be set aside immediately. The first is that the state to which the name purgatory is given is part of hell and the condition of damnation. It is not uncommon to hear people, often well-educated people, using the word as a synonym for hell. Nothing could be further from the truth. It is, unfortunately, a fact that there have been Christian writers and preachers who have so concentrated on the pains and punishments of the purgatorial state that there seems to be very little difference between being in hell and being in purgatory; but even these have recognised that there is no connection between those who have passed through the gates of death in purgatory and those poor, lost souls who in their rejection of God find themselves cut off from the source of love and joy. That latter state is the experience of damnation; but to be in purgatory is already to be in a state of grace and salvation. It is, if one is driven to use picturè-language, the ante-chamber to heaven. There may be pain, but it is the kind of pain that a twisted and crooked body might feel as it is firmly but gently straightened and healed. Moreover, and this is the important point, the pain is gladly accepted and endured, for it is the pain we experience when we approach beauty and truth; the pain of drawing near the fire of the divine love that burns away the self-centred illusions we have of ourselves.

The second misconception is more difficult to eliminate because, unlike the belief that purgatory is a kind of lesser hell, it is not based upon a mistake, and even came to be built into the teaching of the Church of Rome. This is to regard purgatory as a process that goes on after death in a kind of temporal succession which is similar to the process (hence all that talk of the amount of time one could spend in it) we live through on earth. The temptation to take the language of metaphor more literally than was intended is always present and occasionally, as in the case of purgatory, the Church succumbs, despite the warnings of wise leaders and even, sometimes, Councils. In 1563 a decree of the Council of Trent issued a stern warning against the teaching of 'things that belong to the realm of curiosity and superstition', yet an over-literal interpretation of purgatory as a process in time continued to be taught.

That Council, called originally in 1545, set about the task of reforming the Catholic Church and defining its doctrines. It was there that belief in purgatory achieved full dogmatic status:

> The Catholic Church, instructed by the Holy Spirit and in accordance with Sacred Scripture and the ancient Tradition of the Fathers, has taught in the Holy Councils and most recently in this ecumenical Council that there is a purgatory, and that the souls detained there are helped by the acts of intercession (*suffragia*) of the faithful, and especially by the acceptable sacrifice of the altar. Therefore this holy Council commands the bishops to strive diligently that the sound doctrine of purgatory, handed down by the Holy Fathers and the sacred Councils, be believed by the faithful and that it be adhered to, taught and preached everywhere.[1]

But the idea of purgatory, in some form or other, goes back to the earliest days of the Church; and it is rooted, not in intellectual curiosity about what exactly happens to human beings after death, but in the conviction that the living could and should pray for the dead. This practice of prayers for the dead had its antecedents in Judaism. In 2 Maccabees 12 there is the famous account of the war-leader Judas Maccabeus making an offering to the Lord on behalf of the dead.

Unfortunately, there is no space, here, to trace the history of the doctrine of purgatory in Christianity. It is long and fascinating and could be said to have its first documentation in a remarkable and moving piece of writing which comes from the first decade of the third century of the North African Church. It is called *The Passion of Perpetua and Felicitas*[2] and in it the martyr, Perpetua, tells of a vision she has had of her dead brother and the certain knowledge she has that her prayers have helped to heal and save him. Although there was a good deal of hesitation about the exact nature of the 'intermediate' state, the practice of prayers for the dead was universal until the time of the Reformation in the sixteenth century. It is true that there was some conflict with Greek Orthodox Christians in the later

Middle Ages, but not on the basic issue. The Eastern Christians objected, as they nearly always did, to the elaborate definitions of the Western scholars. Their custom of praying for the dead hardly differed, but the speculative delight in the topography of purgatory was of little interest, and indeed rather offensive to the spirit of Byzantine Christianity. The noun *'purgatorium'* does not appear even in the West until the late twelfth century, and, according to the French scholar Jacques Le Goff, the person who integrated the idea into a theological scheme was a man, delightfully named, Peter the Chanter who died in 1197 and was a master of the school of Notre Dame in Paris. He specifically taught that 'the good either go at once to paradise if they have nothing with them to burn, or they go first to purgatory and then to paradise, as in the case of those who bring venial sins with them.'[3]

In the sixteenth century, however, the Protestant reformers totally rejected the notion of purgatory - Calvin called it 'a deadly fiction of Satan which nullifies the cross of Christ'[4] - chiefly on the grounds that it threatened the scriptural teaching that salvation came by faith in Christ alone. The doctrine of purgatory, to them, looked suspiciously like a doctrine of works and merits i.e. a doctrine which held that salvation could be earned, if one worked hard enough at it; that entry into heaven could be gained as a reward after paying the proper price of penitence and pain. But there was more to their rejection than that. There is, sadly, plenty of evidence of the ways in which the idea of purgatory was used as a weapon by a corrupt and unscrupulous Church. What appalled Martin Luther and many of his contemporaries who remained loyal to Rome, was not only the vulgar commercialisation of religion by the sale of indulgences, but the use of the doctrine to enable the clergy to obtain power in another way. As the Middle Ages progressed, the teaching on purgatory that the relief of souls in the after-life required the special intervention of the Church, usually in the form of masses for the dead, enabled the hierarchy to extend and tighten its control over the laity.

It was a sorry state of affairs, yet, despite all the perversions and corruptions and the fantastical elaborations of teachers and preachers, the nobility and humanity of the concept remained intact. That it did so, owed much to the genius of a man whose imagination gave to the world one of its greatest works of art: Dante Alighieri. His long poem, *The Divine Comedy,* is, at its simplest, the story of the journey of a man through hell, purgatory and heaven to attain the sight of God. In many ways the second stage of the journey, up the great mountain of purgatory, where the souls are being purified, is the most moving part of the whole poem. The souls whom Dante and his companion Vergil meet there seem more human. They seem closer to us in their pains and strivings, their hope and urgency. They are in a state of movement towards the blessed light of heaven: there is pain, but there is also hope and longing, and a feeling of joyful anticipation. No one has emphasised more strongly and conveyed more vividly than Dante the truth at the heart of the doctrine, that purgatory is the road to heaven and ultimate happiness. After their journey through the horrors of hell: the stench, the darkness, the cruel silence and the terrible cold, Dante and Vergil awake to find themselves on a beach where the air is clear, the breeze drifts softly off the sea, and the sky is blue above them. A sense of lightness and joy immediately fills them: they are in purgatory, at the foot of a mountain bathed in sunlight. Dante makes the dead forms of the doctrine live and breathe, arousing and satisfying our imaginations by the power of his artistry. Yet the doctrine is there still: the basic medieval teaching that guilt incurred by sin which normally leads to condemnation can be pardoned through contrition and confession, while the punishment is effaced by 'satisfaction' i.e. by completing ones penance. If contrition has taken place but penance not yet been done or completed, then the expiation must take place in purgatory. These are the bones of the formal and abstract doctrine that Dante clothed with such imaginative splendour. Before Dante and Vergil begin their ascent of the terraces of purgatory proper, they climb three stairs: one is white, the symbol of confession, the second is dark purple symbolising contrition, and the last is blazing red to symbolise satisfaction. The question for us is whether the doctrine still has meaning for us and can live in our world. If it cannot, do we follow the leaders of the Protestant Reformation and abandon prayers for the dead too? And how, then, does Dante's great work speak to us?.

First of all, we can, and must, like Dante and the orthodox teachers of the Church, rid ourselves of a crude 'accountancy' theory of purgatory. This is more difficult than it might seem, for we live in a world and a society which insists that debts must be paid, and what is right and fair in daily life is often seen to be right and fair in religion. But to believe that there is an exact payment for each transgression and that God keeps accounts is a violation of the belief in God's forgiveness and a distortion of the basis of Christianity: the assurance that redemption is achieved by the action of God in Christ and that we are justified by faith. But while holding fast to those truths of the gospel we need not abandon the notion of personal responsibility for our thoughts and actions; we have to face the consequences of our choices. And it is this notion of personal responsibility that the doctrine of purgatory greatly enriches. However, this must not lead to the nonsense of encouraging a belief that after death, in purgatory, we are given a second chance to put right what we had rejected or destroyed in life. Quite the contrary: the decisions we make in this life have eternal consequences, and the kind of history we create for ourselves in relation to our given, earthly circumstances is the forging of our identity as a human being. That identity is not dissolved in death, as though we were drops of water being absorbed into the sea; we shall, after death, be recognisably ourselves even though transformed by the love and justice of our creator: that is the promise of 'the resurrection of the body'. The process of that transformation, which is a progress to perfection, might as well be called purgatory as anything else.

In a letter to one of his close friends, the poet and novelist, Charles Williams wrote: 'I am convinced that there must be a Redemption of Sin. It is not enough to leave either personal or public sins behind . . . This, all this, must be known in the good . . .As far as "something after death" goes I believe in two things. I believe that every soul experiences and understands fully the entire and living Justice of the universe. I believe that

Justice to be a living, responsive and intelligent Existence – and one with Almighty Love. And I believe It makes Itself clear to every soul in the way that the soul chooses . . . and . . because Justice-in-Love exists, I believe in a Judgement, an Accounting. Or, to put it another way, I believe that we shall see our thoughts, words and actions in that lucid Justice – that the past lives there, and we shall jolly well know it, where we have sinned and where not, and so on. And this means – if we are to know . . . God and ourselves, some state in which we shall do it . . ."[5] A belief in that 'state' only makes sense if we take seriously *both* our personal responsibility as free creatures *and* the justice of the God who gave us that freedom. The point is this: most of us fumble our way through life and blunder across the border of death; a mixture of fears and doubts, hope and faith. Who would ever argue that we were complete, as human beings, when we die? What about the long list of incidents in our lives: things undone and things done to others' hurt; hatreds, jealousies, meannesses, acts of spite and selfishness? Do these get erased as we die, as if, in God's forgiving love, they did not matter? How would this demonstrate his justice? And would this be what we, as free creatures in the possession of the precious gift of the capacity of self-knowledge, want? Does not true humanity mean knowing and coming to terms with our past? Is not Charles Williams correct: that we are to understand the living justice of the universe, and that this means that all that we are and have been will be known and perceived in that 'lucid Justice'?

In truth, nothing is ignored or passed over: everything must be faced, recognised, known and woven into the pattern of redeemed existence beyond death. We are, as I have said, most of us, poor, incomplete creatures when we die, hence there can be a full ripening and achievement of ourselves only after death. It is precisely that which we shall want: a complete realisation of our personalities. Purgatory, therefore, is not to be thought of as something imposed upon us extrinsically by a God who is determined to make us pay for our sins: it is a condition and a process which we shall need and ardently desire. The forgiveness of God is offered by him freely and utterly, there is no question of us having to earn it; but we have to want it and be capable of receiving it and, in receiving it, experience it as joy. This is what our recalcitrant, self-centred natures find hard: though we are creatures made for joy we tend to resist it, preferring to live in a kind of glumness that is born out of dissatisfaction and envy. When Dante reaches the earthly paradise at the top of the mountain of purgatory he is met by his beloved Beatrice who greets him with words that astonish him. 'How,' she asks him, 'did you dare ascend this mountain? Did you not know that man is happy here?' She does not say that paradise is the dwelling of the good or the holy, but of the happy. Where is purgatory? We may not be able to 'locate' it, but we know that it is the 'place', 'state' or 'process' in which freely, accepting the fire of the divine love, our whole selves learn what it is to experience true joy.

Brian Horne is an honorary assistant priest at St Mary's and a lecturer in Christian doctrine at King's College, London.

Afterword

Graham Leonard

'THE BODY WAS CREATED in such wise that the Word of God
might lay hold of it and assume it; and because the Word was
made flesh the body's condition was therefore changed. It is
redeemed. It awaits its glorification.'[1] These splendid words of
Jean Mouroux express admirably the context provided by the
scriptures as a whole within which the resurrection of Christ
must be considered. We are free, if we will, to reject that context
and to adopt another view of man, his nature and his purpose,
and within that view to examine the resurrection narratives. If
we do so, we must not be surprised if we encounter difficulties
for we shall be examining them in a way which is alien to their
nature.

If we examine any organism, any instrument, we must do so
on the basis of the purpose for which it is designed. If we
consider a person, it must be on the basis of what he or she
professes to be and hopes to achieve. If we examine them on the
basis of what we think they ought to be, our study will not reveal
the truth about them. The life of a politician, for example, can
be examined to see how successful he was in pursuing his
professed political aims or those of his party. The person
conducting the examination need not necessarily be sympathetic
to his aims or believe them to be right but if he is to treat the
politician with integrity, he must judge him by what he professes
to be. If he attempts to use the politician's life as material for
demonstrating that his aims were wrong, he must, nevertheless,
accept unless he has clear evidence to the contrary that the
politician was acting in good faith and not out of cynical
expediency or other unworthy motives.

It is, of course, proper and right for scholars to examine critically the gospel accounts of the resurrection. This is a necessary activity, partly because God has created us with minds which we have a duty to use, partly because the Holy Spirit uses fallible men as they are and does not turn them into mere channels or puppets, and partly because such activity enables us to understand what the writers were intending to convey. But it is also necessary for scholars to examine the assumptions with which they approach the material. It is sometimes evident that objections are raised to the gospel narratives and to their plain meaning not because of difficulties in the accounts themselves but because what they are trying to convey does not accord with assumptions derived from elsewhere than the scriptures.

If this be so, then the proper course is for such scholars to admit openly that their objections are essentially to the underlying beliefs of the biblical writers and to argue against them, rather than to allow the impression to be given that they spring simply from a 'scientific' examination of the documents. Too often the assumption is made without question that contemporary ideas or those of the Enlightenment are true and that the scriptures can therefore be justifiably interpreted in the light of them.

What then is the context in which the scriptures proclaim the resurrection? To attempt to answer that question fully would demand a survey of the whole of Old Testament thought. There are, however, two fundamental truths which run throughout the Old Testament and which relate particularly to the resurrection. The first is that the God who entered into a covenant relationship with Israel and who established the new covenant in Christ, is the same God who created the universe. That is clear from the opening words of Genesis and the echo of them which is found in the opening words of St John's Gospel. The universe, so created, though wounded and distorted, is intrinsically good. Scripture gives us no warrant for supposing that the purpose of God in creation was to be achieved in a purely spiritual way by the eventual extinction of creation or that the physical universe is but a temporary phenomenon which has no permanent place in God's design.

On the contrary, in the biblical understanding of man, he is given specific spiritual characteristics which are to be fulfilled, not by an escape from the physical world, but by exercising a particular role within it, and which will only be completely fulfilled when the physical world itself is wholly consecrated and glorified. Of the physical world man is an integral part and his true purpose is to be achieved as a person, created mind, body and spirit through and in creation, not in spite of it. To describe man as a highly complex psychosomatic unity is only to express in more modern language what the Old Testament says about man. Man is both spirit and body united in a person. His experience and knowledge of the world is through his body, yet he is capable of transcending it. Man speaks in terms of right and wrong, good and evil, beauty and ugliness, justice and injustice which cannot be deduced from or justified by the physical world alone. Man is at once dependent, not least through his body, on the world and his neighbours, yet he possesses his own individuality and freedom. Even in advanced states of contemplation, it is through and in his body that he experiences the presence and activity of God.

Yet, and this leads us to the second of the truths in the Old Testament, man exists in an ambiguous world, a world which is ordered, infinitely varied, creative and beautiful, but which is also wounded, tragic and demonic. What Guardini has said of water applies to creation as a whole: 'For water is at once gentle and terrible; it refreshes and it kills; it is transparent and full of enigma . . . it is from water, from the evil and perilous elements that can fill us at times with shuddering fear, is born that pure and limpid thing "very useful and precious and chaste".' It is also a world in which the way to life is through death. Our Lord himself reflected this characteristic of the physical world when he spoke of how the corn of wheat must fall into the ground and die if it is not to abide alone.

Man himself shares in these tragic ambiguities but for him the trouble does not lie simply in the impersonal which can at once appear as both destructive and life-giving. For man it lies in that fatal flaw of his will described by St Paul, 'the good that I would I do not and the evil that I would not, that I do.'[2] It is this flaw which leads to the distortion of his good and natural instincts, so that compassion becomes condonation, zeal becomes fanaticism, the desire to rest becomes sloth and the admiration of the good becomes envy. Man's body is affected as well as his spirit. It is both noble and can be a misery. It can be resistant and opaque to the experience of the good. The body can revolt against the soul, so that either the soul is dragged down and overwhelmed by the body, or in a way which denies the essential goodness of the body, can try to escape and behave as if man's salvation lay in its rejection.

The Old Testament affirms that the pattern to be found in the physical world, namely that death is the way to life, applies also to man. Sacrifice is at the heart of human life and love. Though there is a place for the application of human effort aimed at steady improvement, that is not enough and because of the flaw in man's nature, he will always tend to respond in a perverse way to attempts to help him whether by legislation, planning, administration or by the simple act of a neighbour, however wise and well-intentioned. We have to learn to die to live, to give that we may receive, whether, for example, by dying to a bachelor existence to rise as a husband sharing life with a wife, or dying to self-sufficiency to live in community. It applies to the whole of our existence, physical and spiritual, and it applies supremely in our relationship to God.

It was within a people steeped in these truths that the Word of God laid hold of a human body and assumed it. He, by whom all things were made, was himself made flesh. It was in and with the body taken of Mary that Jesus accepted the conditions of human existence, including not only temptation, misunderstandings, ridicule, hostility, desertion and ultimately death but also the limitations which bodily existence brings. It was in body, mind and spirit that he lived our humanity for the Father, finally giving himself in the one perfect sacrifice. It was in the body of his flesh, the body taken of Mary, that he broke the power of evil and the nexus of sin. The created world, of which his body was part, was liberated and glorified by his resurrection. In the Bible, God is both the creator of the universe and its redeemer. It is significant that in his magisterial exposition of the gospel in the Epistle to the Romans, St Paul begins with an affirmation of God as creator before writing of what God has done in Christ. The evangelists wrote their accounts of the resurrection against this Old Testament understanding of man, his purpose and nature. To suggest that, when St Luke says that the disciples do not find the body of the Lord Jesus when they entered the tomb, he was merely expressing in a symbolical way the truth that the spirit of Jesus survived death, is not merely to question his veracity; it is to attribute a way of thinking to St Luke which is quite alien to that of the earliest Christians who saw the gospel as fulfilling the Old Testament.

To see the resurrection as no more than a spiritual experience is to abandon the biblical understanding and to pronounce a decree absolute between spirit and matter. Such an attitude conflicts both with the biblical teaching and, being based on an outdated positivism, with the modern scientific understanding of man as a psychosomatic unity.

St Paul says, 'If Christ be not risen, then is our preaching vain and your faith is also vain.' The resurrection is at the heart of the apostolic preaching, and our faith in the gospel which it proclaims calls us not to examine it in the light of the ideas of this or any subsequent century but to allow it to judge us that we may see creation and ourselves in the light of God's revelation.

In a sense, we experience two lives between our baptism and our death, two lives, the one in Christ, the other in Adam. We experience both bodily in terms of our existence as human beings, not one spiritual or mental and the other physical. The one is given by physical birth – that in Adam. The other is given by sacramental birth – that in Christ. The one fulfils and transcends the other. In our physical death we experience the natural end of our life in Adam, but our sacramental life in Christ continues. Our physical body is returned to the created universe from which it came and of which it has always been part. But it returns to a created universe which has been redeemed in Christ in his resurrection, of which by virtue of our sacramental life we shall partake.

The challenge of the resurrection is not new. Men and women have, throughout the ages, found it difficult and too demanding to live truly as human beings, and have been tempted to lapse into either an angelism which sees the spiritual as an escape from the material or into a materialism which in the long run has no better message than 'eat, drink and be merry for tomorrow we die'. The resurrection of Christ calls us to accept the challenge so to live that we may be fulfilled in the whole of our human nature in and for God.

Graham Leonard is Bishop of London.

Notes

The keystone of Christian faith (pages 9-24)

1. Some of the points discussed in this article are treated more fully by the author in his paperback *Christian Hope* (Mowbrays, 1978)
2. E.L. Mascall *Jesus – Who He Is and How We Know Him* (Darton, Longman and Todd, 1985) p.50
3. Origen *Contra Celsum* (Cambridge University Press, 1965) p.281
4. G. P. Fedotov *A Treasury of Russian Spirituality* (Sheed and Ward. 1950) p.84
5. *Ibid.* p.274
6. Richard Rolle *The Fire of Love* (Penguin, 1972) p.45; see also p.93
7. H. U. von Balthasar *The Glory of the Lord* (T. and T. Clark, 1982) pp. 365-425
8. St Augustine *Confessions* X, 6
9. G. Vermes *Jesus the Jew* (Collins, 1970) p.41
10. G. Kaufman *Systematic Theology* (Scribner, 1968) p.425
11. In his book *Jesus – An Experiment in Christology* (Collins, 1979)

The resurrection in liturgical life in the Orthodox church (pages 24-39)

1. Metropolitan Nikodimos of Attica *Gathered together in the Eucharist* (Athens, 1978, in Greek) pp.125-6
2. Great Kanon of St Andrew of Crete, Ode 9
3. Metropolitan George (Khodre) of Mount Lebanon 'Liturgy and Liberation', in *The Near East School of Theology Theological Review* 11/2 (1979) p.10
4. Metropolitan Nikodimos *op. cit.* p.140
5. Archimandrite Vasileios, Abbot of Stavronikita on the Holy Mountain, *Hymn of Entry* (New York, 1984) p.67
6. Metropolitan Nikodimos *op. cit.* p.152
7. Metropolitan George *loc. cit.*
8. i.e. Psalms 3, 37/38, 62/63, 87/88, 102/103, 142/143; where two numbers are given for a Psalm, the first represents the Greek Septuagint numbering used in the Orthodox church and the second the Hebrew numbering found in most English translations.
9. Translations of liturgical texts are based where possible on those of *The Lenten Triodion,* translated by Mother Mary and Archimandrite Kallistos Ware (London, 1978)
10. Metropolitan Nikodimos *op. cit.* p.11
11. Archimandrite Vasileios *op. cit.* pp.67, 69
12. Metropolitan Nikodimos *op. cit.* p.135

13. cf. Easter Kanon, Ode 1
14. Christos Yannaras *The Freedom of Morality* (New York, 1984) p.110
15. After Vespers on Forgiveness Sunday. it is customary to sing the Easter troparion quietly while people go up to ask each other's forgiveness.
16. This actually has its place in the Typika, the office which, in Lent, comes between the Ninth Hour and Vespers with the Liturgy of the Presanctified.
17. *On the Formation of Man;* Migne *Patrologia Graeca* 44:188
18. The Kanon is a long poem of nine sections or Odes, each based on a scriptural Ode (e.g. the Ninth is based on the Magnificat). The *eirmos* is the first verse of each Ode; it normally forms a link between the Scriptural Ode and the Kanon, and sets a pattern for the following troparia or verses of that Ode.
19. Verses for Matins of Holy Friday; like all the Holy Week services, this service is anticipated. It is celebrated on Thursday evening.
20. Metropolitan Nikodimos *op. cit.* p.157
21. Theodoret of Cyr *Festive Epistle* 64; *Sources Chrétiens* 98, p.144
22. Liturgy of St Basil
23. Lauds, Holy Saturday Matins (Friday evening)
24. Protopresbyter Michael Kardamakis 'The Cross, judgement of our judgement' in *The Cross and Resurrection* (Athens, 1984, in Greek) p.95
25. Homily read on Easter night, attributed to St John Chrysostom.
26. St Isaac the Syrian, Logos 54; *Ascetic Works* ed. Spetsieris (Athens, 1895, reprinted Thessaloniki, 1977) p.216

The resurrection in some modern novels (pages 40-55)

1. Iris Murdoch *The Good Apprentice* (Chatto and Windus, 1985) p.147
2. Iris Murdoch *The Sovereignty of Good* (Routledge and Kegan Paul, 1970)
3. As, for example, in W Marxsen, *The Resurrection of Jesus of Nazareth* (S.C.M., 1970)
4. Leo Tolstoy *Resurrection* (F. R. Henderson, 1900) p.564
5. Dostoevsky *Crime and Punishment* (Penguin, 1951) p.559
6. *Ibid.* pp.341-2
7. Patrick White *Riders in the Chariot* (Penguin,˙1974) p.484
8. *Ibid.* pp.491-2
9. *Ibid.* pp.426-7
10. Philippians 3,8-11
11. *Riders in the Chariot* p.423
12. *Ibid.* p.453
13. *Ibid.* p.492
14. William Golding *Darkness Visible* (Faber, 1979) p.19
15. *Ibid.* p.43
16. *Ibid.* p.263
17. D. H. Lawrence 'The Man who Died' in *Love among the Haystacks and other stories* (Penguin, 1960) pp.166-7

18. *Ibid.* p.170
19. Edwin Muir 'The Annunciation' *Collected Poems* (Faber, 1960) p.117
20. R. C. Hutchinson *Rising* (Michael Joseph, 1976) pp.212-30, 353
21. *Ibid.* p.359
22. R. C. Hutchinson *Johanna at Daybreak* (Michael Joseph, 1969)
23. Amongst those concerned simply with the crucifixion or its reenactment might be singled out *Christ Recrucified* and *The Last Temptation* by Nikos Kazantzakis, both published by Faber.
24. As, for example, in the Church of the Chora in Istanbul.

Did Jesus really rise from the dead? (pages 56-66)
1. S.P.C.K., 1984
2. S.C.M. Press, 1977, edited by John Hick
3. *The Resurrection of Jesus.* p.122
4. *Ibid.* p.123
5. *Ibid.* p.125
6. *Ibid.* p.128
7. *Ibid.* p.129
8. *Ibid.* p.130 ff
9. *Ibid.* p.152
10. *Ibid.* p.142
11. *Ibid.* p.146
12. Exeter, Paternoster Press, 1984
13. *op. cit.* p.99
14. *Easter Enigma* p.11
15. *The Man Born to be King* (Gollancz, 1943) p.35
16. *Easter Enigma* p.10,11
17. *Ibid.* p.124 ff
18. *Ibid,* p.122
19. Appendix III
20. *Ibid.* p.122 ff
21. Ephesians 1.20; 2.6

The soul of man (pages 72-81)
1. See Penguin edition
2. Now available as a book *Freud and Man's Soul* (Fontana, 1985)
3. Michael Scammell *Solzhenitsyn : a biography* (Hutchinson, 1985)
4. John L. McKenzie *Dictionary of the Bible* (Chapman, 1966)
5. John Hick *Death and Eternal Life* (Macmillan, 1985)
6. Paul Badham *Dictionary of Christian Theology* (S.C.M., 1983)

Where is purgatory? (pages 92-100)
1. *The Christian Faith in the Doctrinal Documents of the Catholic Church* ed. J. Neuner and T. Dupuis (Collins, 1983)
2. See Jacques Le Goff *The Birth of Purgatory* (Scolar Press, 1984)

3. *Ibid.* p.165
4. *Institutes of the Christian Religion,* III,5,vi-x (Eerdmans, 1983)
5. Quoted by Alice Mary Hadfield in *Charles Williams : An Exploration of His Life and Work* (O.U.P., 1983) pp.230-1

Afterword (pages 101-106)
1. *The Meaning of Man* (Sheed and Ward, 1948)
2. Romans 7.19